This book is dedicated to all those who are excited about
working together to make changes in assessment and
evaluation that will help us better support learners.

TOGETHER IS BETTER

COLLABORATIVE ASSESSMENT, EVALUATION & REPORTING

ANNE DAVIES · CAREN CAMERON
COLLEEN POLITANO · KATHLEEN GREGORY

PEGUIS PUBLISHERS
WINNIPEG · CANADA

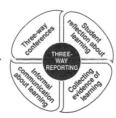

Printed and bound in Canada by Hignell Printing Limited

96   95   94   93   5   4   3   2

Canadian Cataloguing in Publication Data
Main entry under title:

Together is better

   Includes bibliographical references.
   ISBN 1-895411-54-8

1. Language experience approach in education –
Evaluation.   2. Teaching – Evaluation.
3. Parent-teacher relationships.   I. Davies, Anne, 1955–

LB1576.T63 1992   372.6044   C92-098161-5

Book and Cover Design: Laura Ayers
Cover Illustration: Jess Dixon

Peguis Publishers Ltd.
520 Hargrave Street
Winnipeg, MB
Canada R3A 0X8

Contents

Introduction

Part I What Is Three-Way Reporting?

1. **Three-Way Reports**   7

   A Snapshot of the Preparation of Three-Way Reports   8
   Learning from Listening   17
   Three-Way Reporting—Keeping Focused   19
   Three-Way Reporting—Together Is Better   21

   Part II The Three-Way Reporting Process Unfolds

2. **Three-Way Conferences**   25

   A Snapshot of the Three-Way Conferencing Process   26
   A Typical Three-Way Conference—Mackenzie's Story   27
   Three-Way Conferencing—Teacher-Proven Ideas   30
     Idea! Playing with Possibilities   31
     Idea! Helping Parents Prepare for the Conference   32
     Idea! Working Out the Wrinkles   33
     Idea! Providing a Safe Audience   35
     Idea! Providing a Conference Guide for Teachers   36
     Idea! Providing a Conference Guide for Students   37
     Idea! Setting Student Goals   38
     Idea! Going Further with Goal Setting   39
     Idea! Reflecting on Three-Way Conferencing   40
     Idea! Inviting Feedback   41
   Learning from Listening   42
   Three-Way Conferencing—Keeping Focused   44
   Three-Way Conferencing—Together Is Better   46

3. **Informal Communication**   47

   A Snapshot of Informal Communication: A Page
     from the Album   48

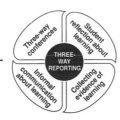

Informal Communication—Teacher-Proven Ideas   49
   Idea! Capturing Student Learning   50
   Idea! Viewing a Video   51
   Idea! Inviting Parent Response   52
   Idea! Providing Viewing Guidelines for Parents   53
   Idea! Demonstrating Progress   54
   Idea! Showing What We Know   55
   Idea! Informal Reports to Parents   57
   Idea! Making a Birthday Call   61
   Idea! Getting Information from Parents   62
   Idea! Giving Parents an Active Learning Experience   63
Learning from Listening   64
Informal Communication—Keeping Focused   65
Informal Communication—Together Is Better   66

4. **Evidence of Learning**   67

A Snapshot of "Evidence of Learning"   68
Evidence of Learning—Teacher-Proven Ideas   69
   Idea! Showing Your Knowledge   70
   Idea! Brainstorming Evidence of Learning   71
   Idea! Recording Activities Done at Learning Centers   72
   Idea! Constructing a Whole-Class Question-and-
        Answer Grid   73
   Idea! Thinking About Writing   74
   Idea! Setting Challenges for Finding Evidence   75
   Idea! Getting Parents to Provide Evidence of Learning   76
   Idea! Modeling for the Class   77
   Idea! Using Criteria   78
   Idea! Improving the Selection of Work for
        Students' Collections   79
Learning from Listening   80
Collecting Evidence of Learning—Keeping Focused   82
Evidence of Learning—Together Is Better   84

5. **Student Reflection**   85

A Snapshot of Student Reflection   86
Student Reflection—Teacher-Proven Ideas   87
   Idea! Modeling Reflection for Your Students   88
   Idea! Providing for Oral Rehearsal   89
   Idea! Reflecting with a Partner   90

Idea! Encouraging Student Self-reflection   91
Idea! Getting Specific   92
Idea! Recording Reflections   93
Idea! Adding to the Collections of Students' Work   94
Idea! Including Parents   95
Idea! Recording Memorable Moments   96
Idea! Giving Specific Compliments   97
Idea! The Week in Review   98
Learning from Listening   99
Student Reflection—Keeping Focused   100
Student Reflection—Together Is Better   101

Conclusion: Creating a Collaborative Environment   103

Appendix A   Anecdotal Reports   105
Appendix B   Suggested Resources   109
Appendix C   Blackline Masters   111

Acknowledgments

We are most appreciative of the individual and collective contributions of staff members at Wishart, David Cameron, and Sangster elementary schools in School District #62, Sooke, British Columbia, for their work with anecdotal reporting and informal reporting.

We would like to give particular thanks to the staff, students, and parents of Tsolum Elementary School in School District #71, Courtenay, British Columbia, who allowed us to be part of their learning as they took risks and worked to develop three-way conferencing and three-way reporting:

Leslie Bell, Lisa Brown, Darlene Burns, Beverly Clarke, Vicki Dreger, Stewart Duncan, Al Dzuba, Gwyn Epp, Shirley Evans, Heather Ferraby, Al Fraser, Brian Goodwin, Bruce Gordon, Kathy Gotto, John Harrison, Jane Hunter, Sylvia Hurford, Jan Hyham, Corrine Innes, Janice Isenor, Hans Jorgensen, Elaine Kierstead, Leslie Krainer, Wendy Laing, Mike Laughlin, Valerie Machin, Marina Mahabir, Jill Olsson, Joanne O'Toole, Darry Oudendag, Susan Sandland, Charles Schellinck, Margaret Thran, Rosemary Vernon, Mary Weiler.

Introduction

There are many different ways of assessing and evaluating children's work and preparing to report to parents. Teachers today are using and developing numerous innovative strategies to make their assessment, evaluation, and reporting more manageable for themselves and more effective for students and their parents.

This book is for elementary teachers. It describes three-way reporting [among teacher, parents, child] and the collaborative processes that support it. For each of the four supporting processes—three-way conferences, informal communication, collecting evidence of learning, student reflection on their learning—we offer definitions, descriptions, and examples that have worked for teachers. Since each of the four supporting processes can be used on its own or in combination with the others, teachers may choose to use one or more areas depending on their own comfort level and those of their students and parents. If three-way reporting is your goal, all four supporting components are essential.

Here are the underlying beliefs that have guided our decision-making and our implementation of the processes that lead to collaborative assessment, evaluation, and reporting.

We know that people learn not only by themselves but also by working with others.

Therefore...
Teachers need to work together to plan changes, knowing that there is more than one "right" way to involve students and parents in evaluating and reporting collaboratively.

We know that people's ability to learn is directly related to how they feel about themselves.

Therefore...

We need to help teachers talk through the issues relating to reporting. Teachers need time to understand the process and to gain confidence in their ability to work collaboratively with students and parents.

We know that people have an infinite capacity to learn.

Therefore...

We need to allow collaborative reporting to evolve as we learn. The more we learn, the more the reporting process will change. Teachers need to be able to think of changes in reporting not as finding the one "best" way to report but rather as finding the process that enables their reporting practices to best enhance student learning.

We know that people construct their own knowledge through activity and experience.

Therefore...

We recognize that none of us has all the answers. It is important that teachers create the reporting process that makes sense for them, their students, and their students' parents. In one sense, there is no way that we will ever be completely ready for collaborative assessment. Just as learning to write is a never-ending process of refining ideas and skills, evaluation and reporting are processes that involve continuous learning and relearning.

We know that people learn by making connections between themselves and their world.

Therefore...

Teachers must look at any new process and ask: Does this work for me? How can it enhance learning for my students? How much time can I afford to give to this? What part of this process should I start with? What would I choose to do differently? We encourage you to ask yourself these questions as you examine the ideas presented in this book.

We know that people learn at different rates and in different ways.

Therefore...

We continue to expand the ways that we choose to assess, evaluate, and report student learning in ways that enhance learning. We are all at different places—all on a continuum of learning.

This book is about learning—for children, for teachers, for parents. As teachers, we need to remind ourselves that our teaching practice is always a work-in-progress—changing, adapting, improving. If we had waited until we knew everything there was to know about evaluation and reporting, we would never have written this book. Therefore, we invite you to work with your students, their parents, and your colleagues to develop reporting processes that support learning and that work for you.

This book describes reporting that emphasizes the collaboration of students, parents, and teachers at each stage of the reporting process. We invite you into this process because we've found that working **TOGETHER IS BETTER.**

PART I

What Is Three-Way Reporting?

Three-Way Reports

Educators are always searching for ways to provide written reports for parents that are in alignment with their beliefs about learning and learners. One colleague, Sharon Jeroski, cautions, "Until we can make reports to parents purposeful and possible, we'll never be able to make significant changes to our practice." It is out of this search for purposeful and possible written reports that the three-way reporting process has developed, and we have discovered that the process is as valuable as the reports coming out of that process.

Most teachers are required to provide one or more written reports to their students' parents during the course of the school year. Three-way reports are one way of fulfilling this requirement. Traditionally, reports have been written by the teacher and sent to the parents prior to any interview. In contrast, those teachers writing three-way reports write them only *following* the three-way conferences, as a summation of those conferences, which in each case has included the parents, the student, and the teacher. Each of these reports provides a written record of the conference discussion and details each student's areas of strength and concern. Three-way reports conclude with a clear statement of the child's learning goals, and how the parent and teacher will provide support for this learning.

On pages 9 and 10 we illustrate a typical three-way report form and then give you five examples of completed forms.

A SNAPSHOT OF THE PREPARATION OF THREE-WAY REPORTS

1. During each three-way conference, the teacher summarizes and records the discussion.

2. After each three-way conference, the teacher takes a few minutes to complete the conference discussion record sheet.

3. The teacher writes each three-way report based on her notes.

4. The teacher shares each three-way report with the student, asking if anything has been missed or if there is anything the student would like to add. If so, additions are made.

5. After making and filing a photocopy, the teacher sends home each three-way report with an invitation to the parents who attended to add any additional comments.

6. After the parents note any comments, sign, and return the report, the teacher replaces the photocopy in her file with this report.

Below left   see figure 1, p. 9
Below right   see figure 6, p. 36

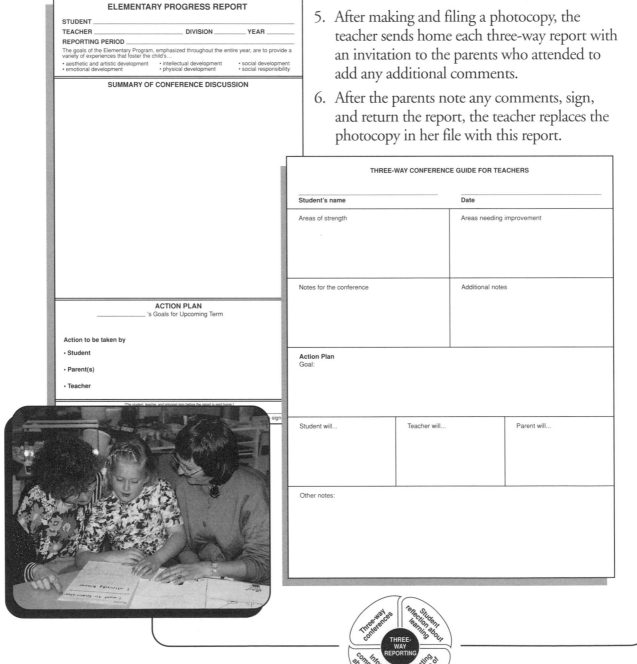

ELEMENTARY PROGRESS REPORT

STUDENT _____

TEACHER _____ DIVISION _____ YEAR _____

REPORTING PERIOD _____

The goals of the Elementary Program, emphasized throughout the entire year, are to provide a variety of experiences that foster the child's...
- aesthetic and artistic development
- emotional development
- intellectual development
- physical development
- social development
- social responsibility

SUMMARY OF CONFERENCE DISCUSSION

ACTION PLAN
_____ 's Goals for Upcoming Term

Action to be taken by
- Student
- Parent(s)
- Teacher

[The student, teacher, and principal sign before the report is sent home.]

THREE-WAY CONFERENCE GUIDE FOR TEACHERS

Student's name _____ Date _____

Areas of strength	Areas needing improvement
Notes for the conference	Additional notes

Action Plan
Goal:

Student will...	Teacher will...	Parent will...

Other notes:

THREE-WAY REPORTING

Three-way conferences · Student reflection about learning · Informal communication about learning · Collecting evidence of learning

Note: This is page one of the report form that is sent home to parents on 8 1/2" x 14" paper.

ELEMENTARY PROGRESS REPORT

STUDENT _____

TEACHER _____ DIVISION _____ YEAR _____

REPORTING PERIOD _____

The goals of the Elementary Program, emphasized throughout the entire year, are to provide a variety of experiences that foster the child's…

- aesthetic and artistic development
- emotional development
- intellectual development
- physical development
- social development
- social responsibility

SUMMARY OF CONFERENCE DISCUSSION

—To be filled in by the teacher following the three-way conference.

Additional comments about the conference from teacher

—To be filled in by the teacher following the three-way conference.

Additional comments about the conference from parent(s) and student

—To be filled in by the parents and student when the report is sent home. Both are, of course, optional.

—To be filled in at the time of the three-way conference.

ACTION PLAN
_____ 's Goals for Upcoming Term

Action to be taken by

- **Student**

- **Parent(s)**

- **Teacher**

[The student, teacher, and principal sign before the report is sent home.]

_____   _____   _____   _____
Student's signature   Teacher's signature   Parent's signature   Principal's signature

Figure 1 Three-Way Report Form—Side One

adapted from progress report form of Tsolum School, Courtenay, B.C. (School District #71)

Note: This is the second page of the report form, on the reverse of page one.

–This space includes the school logo, address, phone number, and school motto.

TERM OVERVIEW

–This section is an overview of the class's program for the term.

PARENT'S COMMENTS

–This section of general comments is filled in by parent(s) when report is sent home.

Figure 1   Three-Way
Report Form—Side Two

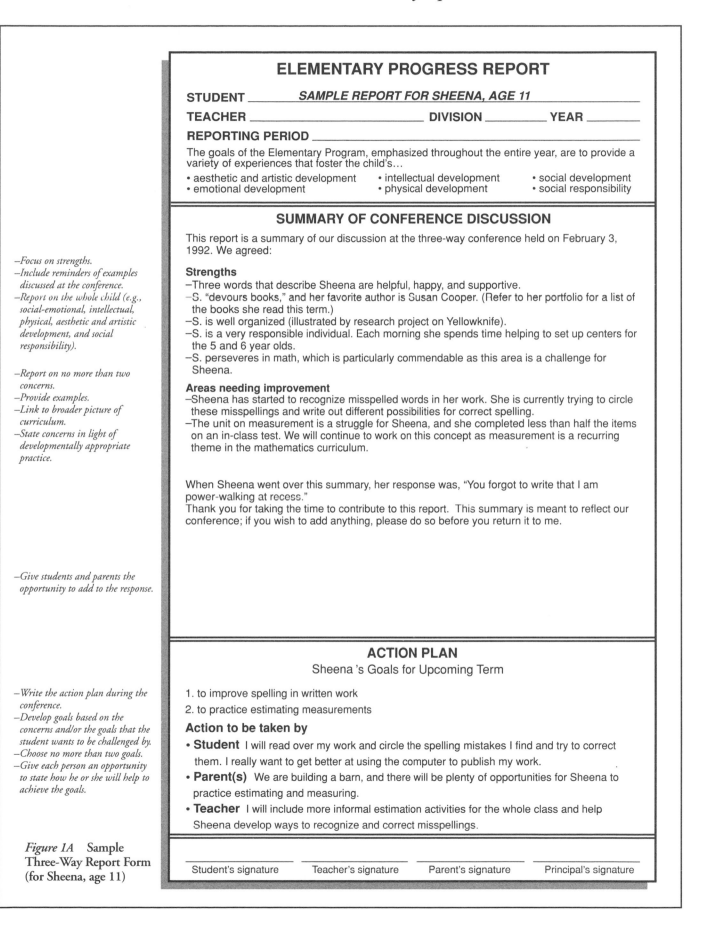

—Focus on strengths.
—Include reminders of examples discussed at the conference.
—Report on the whole child (e.g., social-emotional, intellectual, physical, aesthetic and artistic development, and social responsibility).

—Report on no more than two concerns.
—Provide examples.
—Link to broader picture of curriculum.
—State concerns in light of developmentally appropriate practice.

—Give students and parents the opportunity to add to the response.

—Write the action plan during the conference.
—Develop goals based on the concerns and/or the goals that the student wants to be challenged by.
—Choose no more than two goals.
—Give each person an opportunity to state how he or she will help to achieve the goals.

Figure 1A Sample Three-Way Report Form (for Sheena, age 11)

ELEMENTARY PROGRESS REPORT

STUDENT _____ *SAMPLE REPORT FOR SHEENA, AGE 11* _____

TEACHER _____ DIVISION _____ YEAR _____

REPORTING PERIOD _____

The goals of the Elementary Program, emphasized throughout the entire year, are to provide a variety of experiences that foster the child's…

- aesthetic and artistic development
- emotional development
- intellectual development
- physical development
- social development
- social responsibility

SUMMARY OF CONFERENCE DISCUSSION

This report is a summary of our discussion at the three-way conference held on February 3, 1992. We agreed:

Strengths
—Three words that describe Sheena are helpful, happy, and supportive.
—S. "devours books," and her favorite author is Susan Cooper. (Refer to her portfolio for a list of the books she read this term.)
—S. is well organized (illustrated by research project on Yellowknife).
—S. is a very responsible individual. Each morning she spends time helping to set up centers for the 5 and 6 year olds.
—S. perseveres in math, which is particularly commendable as this area is a challenge for Sheena.

Areas needing improvement
—Sheena has started to recognize misspelled words in her work. She is currently trying to circle these misspellings and write out different possibilities for correct spelling.
—The unit on measurement is a struggle for Sheena, and she completed less than half the items on an in-class test. We will continue to work on this concept as measurement is a recurring theme in the mathematics curriculum.

When Sheena went over this summary, her response was, "You forgot to write that I am power-walking at recess."
Thank you for taking the time to contribute to this report. This summary is meant to reflect our conference; if you wish to add anything, please do so before you return it to me.

ACTION PLAN
Sheena 's Goals for Upcoming Term

1. to improve spelling in written work
2. to practice estimating measurements

Action to be taken by
- **Student** I will read over my work and circle the spelling mistakes I find and try to correct them. I really want to get better at using the computer to publish my work.
- **Parent(s)** We are building a barn, and there will be plenty of opportunities for Sheena to practice estimating and measuring.
- **Teacher** I will include more informal estimation activities for the whole class and help Sheena develop ways to recognize and correct misspellings.

_____   _____   _____   _____
Student's signature   Teacher's signature   Parent's signature   Principal's signature

—Provide the student's own words or work samples.
—Give specific book titles.

—Provide written reminder that this issue is not a new one.

—Read the report to younger children (such as Colby) and obtain their response.

—Ask students to express their goal(s) in their own words, e.g., "How will you know when you're achieving your goal?" "What will I see you doing that will tell me...?"

Figure 1B Sample Three-Way Report Form (for Colby, age 5 years 10 months)

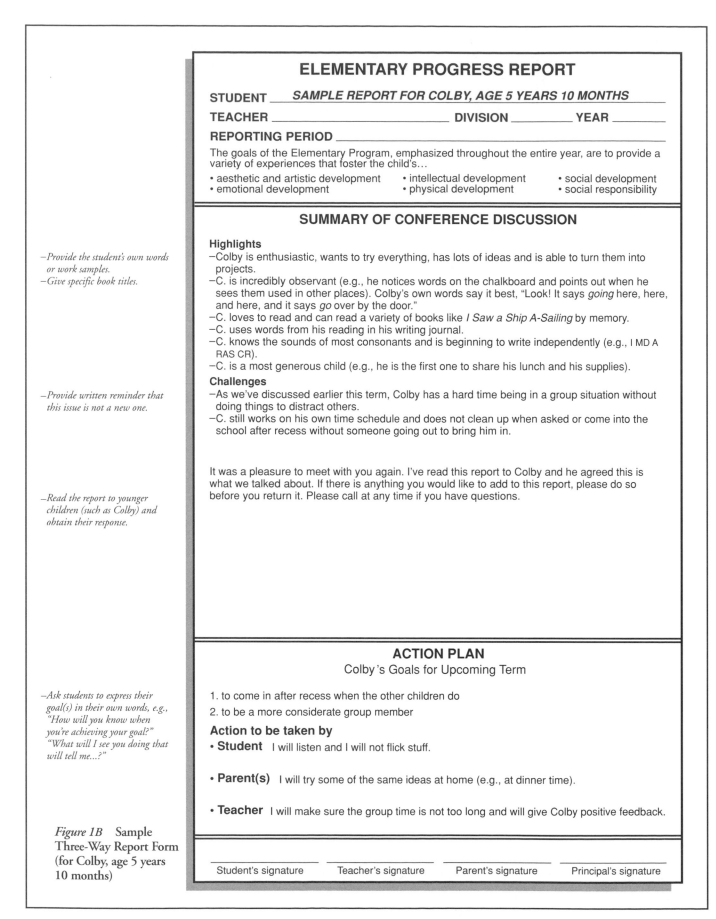

ELEMENTARY PROGRESS REPORT

STUDENT ___*SAMPLE REPORT FOR COLBY, AGE 5 YEARS 10 MONTHS*___

TEACHER _____ DIVISION _____ YEAR _____

REPORTING PERIOD _____

The goals of the Elementary Program, emphasized throughout the entire year, are to provide a variety of experiences that foster the child's...

- aesthetic and artistic development
- emotional development
- intellectual development
- physical development
- social development
- social responsibility

SUMMARY OF CONFERENCE DISCUSSION

Highlights
—Colby is enthusiastic, wants to try everything, has lots of ideas and is able to turn them into projects.
—C. is incredibly observant (e.g., he notices words on the chalkboard and points out when he sees them used in other places). Colby's own words say it best, "Look! It says *going* here, here, and here, and it says *go* over by the door."
—C. loves to read and can read a variety of books like *I Saw a Ship A-Sailing* by memory.
—C. uses words from his reading in his writing journal.
—C. knows the sounds of most consonants and is beginning to write independently (e.g., I MD A RAS CR).
—C. is a most generous child (e.g., he is the first one to share his lunch and his supplies).

Challenges
—As we've discussed earlier this term, Colby has a hard time being in a group situation without doing things to distract others.
—C. still works on his own time schedule and does not clean up when asked or come into the school after recess without someone going out to bring him in.

It was a pleasure to meet with you again. I've read this report to Colby and he agreed this is what we talked about. If there is anything you would like to add to this report, please do so before you return it. Please call at any time if you have questions.

ACTION PLAN
Colby's Goals for Upcoming Term

1. to come in after recess when the other children do
2. to be a more considerate group member

Action to be taken by

- **Student** I will listen and I will not flick stuff.

- **Parent(s)** I will try some of the same ideas at home (e.g., at dinner time).

- **Teacher** I will make sure the group time is not too long and will give Colby positive feedback.

_____ _____ _____ _____
Student's signature   Teacher's signature   Parent's signature   Principal's signature

ELEMENTARY PROGRESS REPORT

STUDENT ___*SAMPLE REPORT FOR MADDY, AGE 7 YEARS 2 MONTHS*___

TEACHER _____ **DIVISION** _____ **YEAR** _____

REPORTING PERIOD _____

The goals of the Elementary Program, emphasized throughout the entire year, are to provide a variety of experiences that foster the child's...

- aesthetic and artistic development
- intellectual development
- social development
- emotional development
- physical development
- social responsibility

SUMMARY OF CONFERENCE DISCUSSION

Strengths

–Maddy met her goal of last term to write at least three sentences in her journal each day.
–Everyone likes Maddy—she is cooperative, helpful, and fits in when doing group work.
–M. doesn't give up easily.
–M. enjoys being read to. For her independent reading, she regularly selects pattern books she is very familiar with (e.g., her favorite continues to be *Mary Wore Her Red Dress* by Merle Peek).
–The effort M. puts into all her work is mind-boggling (e.g., she spends much time on her drawings and printing in her journal).
–Maddy's math work is always carefully done, and she keeps her work well organized.

Focus Areas

–I am concerned about the pace of Maddy's growth in reading and have asked Mr. Lane, the learning assistance teacher, to assist. He will be coming into our class to work with Maddy and some other children next term. Hopefully, this will help her gain more confidence in this important area.

I appreciated the opportunity to meet with you at our conference, and I am looking forward to seeing you again on April 15 when we will review Maddy's reading and the goals we've set. Mr. Lane will join us.

ACTION PLAN
Maddy's Goals for Upcoming Term

1. to read a greater variety of books

Action to be taken by

- **Student**   I'll read more everyday.

- **Parent(s)**   We'll read to Maddy every night that we can.

- **Teacher**   I'll send a variety of books home in a book bag every week, find more books with accompanying tapes to use in class, and work with Mr. Lane to develop a plan to support Maddy's learning.

_____   _____   _____   _____
Student's signature   Teacher's signature   Parent's signature   Principal's signature

–When the child's abilities to do a task are obviously outside developmentally appropriate expectations (vs. grade-level expectations) concerns need to be stated and plans developed.
–Include school support personnel who are working with the child in the concern area.

–Invite parents to have further discussions around these concerns and set the next meeting date to review the goal.

Ensure that the goal is attainable (within the developmental range of the child).

Figure 1C Sample Three-Way Report Form (for Maddy, age 7 years 2 months)

—Record strengths without negating them with "but", "however..."
—Look for strengths beyond the classroom.

—State concerns in clear language.
—Use specific examples.

—Acknowledge student and parent expertise.
—Include others who work with the student.

—Keep goals realistic and possible.

Figure 1D Sample
Three-Way Report Form
(for Jason, age 8)

ELEMENTARY PROGRESS REPORT

STUDENT _____ *SAMPLE REPORT FOR JASON, AGE 8* _____

TEACHER _____ DIVISION _____ YEAR _____

REPORTING PERIOD _____

The goals of the Elementary Program, emphasized throughout the entire year, are to provide a variety of experiences that foster the child's...

• aesthetic and artistic development   • intellectual development   • social development
• emotional development   • physical development   • social responsibility

SUMMARY OF CONFERENCE DISCUSSION

During our three-way conference, we had the opportunity to look at and discuss Jason's collection of work and to talk together about specific strengths and concerns from this first term. This report is a summary of our conversation.

Strengths
—Jason shows enthusiasm for everything that catches his attention.
—J. loves to read a variety of books of his choosing (to find the wide range he needs he regularly goes to the public library on Wednesday with the Library Club).
—J's general knowledge is amazing, and he always wants to share particular facts and information (e.g., he knows everything about space there is to know).
—J. relates well to adults in a one-on-one situation, usually out of the classroom setting.
—J. is quick to understand the concepts presented in math.

Concerns
—Jason finds it next to impossible to work with his peers; this is also a concern at home.
—J. doesn't complete assignments and is reluctant to do homework that requires written work. He seems to have the necessary skills and abilities, and when he works with the learning assistance teacher in a one-on-one setting he produces the required written work. We are struggling to figure out the reasons behind this behavior and how we can help.

We have had several discussions already this year and this conference really highlighted a number of key points. Your honesty and open approach allowed us to talk through some important areas. Having Mrs. Brown, our learning assistance teacher, in attendance also provided valuable insights. But most important were Jason's own comments and willingness to take an honest look at what is going on. If I've missed anything on this report, please add before returning it to school.

ACTION PLAN
Jason's Goals for Upcoming Term

1. to get along with others
2. to get more written work done

Action to be taken by

• **Student** I am going to find one person in our class that I can work with when we have to work with someone else.

• **Parent(s)** We'll get Jason involved in a swimming program with kids his own age.

• **Teacher** I will work with Jason to make sure that a minimum of one written assignment is completed every day. In the beginning I will focus on just "getting it down."

_____   _____   _____   _____
Student's signature   Teacher's signature   Parent's signature   Principal's signature

ELEMENTARY PROGRESS REPORT

STUDENT _____ *SAMPLE REPORT FOR DIVINDER, AGE 10* _____

TEACHER _____ DIVISION _____ YEAR _____

REPORTING PERIOD _____

The goals of the Elementary Program, emphasized throughout the entire year, are to provide a variety of experiences that foster the child's…

• aesthetic and artistic development
• emotional development
• intellectual development
• physical development
• social development
• social responsibility

SUMMARY OF CONFERENCE DISCUSSION

Successes
—Divinder meets every challenge he is presented with.
—D. is a confident, successful reader. He helps in the library at noon.
—D. is a peer tutor who is well respected by his classmates and other students in the school.
—D. takes part in school sports and is a team captain.
—D.'s computer ability enhances many of his projects (e.g., his project on an ocean study was published on the computer and not only met, but exceeded, the criteria—he received 20/20).

Challenges
—Divinder is challenging himself to create a computer game in mathematics this term.
—Each month, D. works with a high school science buddy on a project related to the environment.

It is obvious how valuable your support is to Divinder. Further, the help you provide in this classroom has enhanced the learning of other children. Thank you from all of us. Please add any comments that I may have missed from our conversation.

ACTION PLAN
Divinder's Goals for Upcoming Term

1. to keep up the fine work!!

Action to be taken by

• **Student** I want to keep working with Dave at the high school on our recycling project.

• **Parent(s)** We will give Divinder more time on the computer at home.

• **Teacher** I'll continue to try to find the resources to support your learning, Divinder.

_____ _____ _____ _____
Student's signature   Teacher's signature   Parent's signature   Principal's signature

Margin notes:
—*Use specific examples to help parents "see" what the teacher knows about the student.*

—*Note the opportunities for challenge and enrichment.*

—*Acknowledge home support and encouragement.*

—*Affirm the comprehensive nature of the student's success.*

Figure 1E **Sample Three-Way Report Form (for Divinder, age 10)**

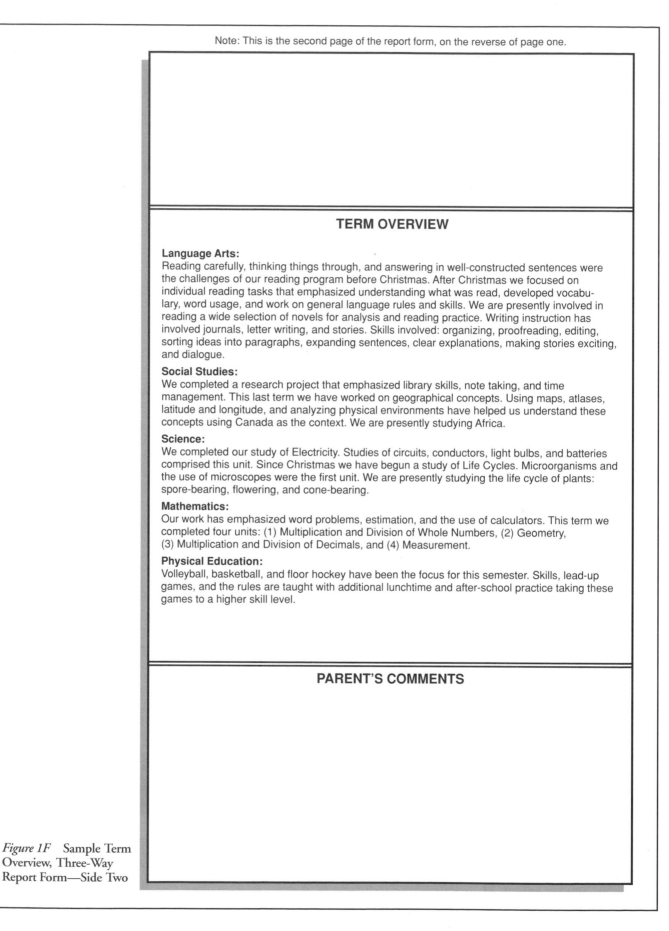

Note: This is the second page of the report form, on the reverse of page one.

TERM OVERVIEW

Language Arts:
Reading carefully, thinking things through, and answering in well-constructed sentences were the challenges of our reading program before Christmas. After Christmas we focused on individual reading tasks that emphasized understanding what was read, developed vocabulary, word usage, and work on general language rules and skills. We are presently involved in reading a wide selection of novels for analysis and reading practice. Writing instruction has involved journals, letter writing, and stories. Skills involved: organizing, proofreading, editing, sorting ideas into paragraphs, expanding sentences, clear explanations, making stories exciting, and dialogue.

Social Studies:
We completed a research project that emphasized library skills, note taking, and time management. This last term we have worked on geographical concepts. Using maps, atlases, latitude and longitude, and analyzing physical environments have helped us understand these concepts using Canada as the context. We are presently studying Africa.

Science:
We completed our study of Electricity. Studies of circuits, conductors, light bulbs, and batteries comprised this unit. Since Christmas we have begun a study of Life Cycles. Microorganisms and the use of microscopes were the first unit. We are presently studying the life cycle of plants: spore-bearing, flowering, and cone-bearing.

Mathematics:
Our work has emphasized word problems, estimation, and the use of calculators. This term we completed four units: (1) Multiplication and Division of Whole Numbers, (2) Geometry, (3) Multiplication and Division of Decimals, and (4) Measurement.

Physical Education:
Volleyball, basketball, and floor hockey have been the focus for this semester. Skills, lead-up games, and the rules are taught with additional lunchtime and after-school practice taking these games to a higher skill level.

PARENT'S COMMENTS

Figure 1F Sample Term Overview, Three-Way Report Form—Side Two

LEARNING FROM LISTENING

As we listen to the comments of students, parents, and teachers, we continue to learn more about the process.

Parent: "I don't know why I ever bothered to come [to the conference] before. It was all there in the report card...there was really nothing to talk about. This time I got to share in my child's learning. I don't ever want to do it any other way."

Parents support changes in reporting when they are involved in the process and have the opportunity to give their suggestions and be heard.

Teacher: "If we'd come to a consensus as a staff before we did this, we wouldn't be having the problems we're having now."

Staff discussion time is essential. We need opportunities to talk about staff beliefs and values concerning reporting before formulating plans.

Student: "I really liked having my mom and dad there. I felt kinda nervous but it was neat to show them my stuff."

We need to support and guide our students through every step of a new process.

Teacher: "I wish I had spent more time getting ready for the conference. Next time my kids will be better prepared. They had so much to say that I hated to cut them off, but they would have gone on for hours! Next time they'll have their key points prepared, and so will I."

In-class time for rehearsal with a classmate or an older student from another class helps students prepare for the conference. Preparation time is crucial for the success of the process.

Teacher: "I had no idea how anxious many of the parents were. Our parents asked for help—they wanted to be ready for the conference too. I was surprised. I hadn't thought they needed any help."

We need to inform and involve our students' parents in every possible way.

Parent: "I liked the fact that I understood exactly what the teacher was saying about my child's development and her weaknesses because they had been discussed earlier during the conference."

Face-to-face discussion is often the best forum for clear communication.

THREE-WAY REPORTING—KEEPING FOCUSED

TEACHER CONSIDERATIONS	RESPONSE
1. How have I involved the students in the process of three-way reporting? ✐ Are students ready for the three-way conference?	

2. How have I involved the parents in the process of three-way reporting?
 	
  ✐ Have we talked about what usually happens during a three-way conference?
  ✐ How have I helped parents prepare their questions and suggestions?
  ✐ How have I invited parent responses?
  ✐ How have I incorporated parents' suggestions?
  ✐ How am I planning to find out whether their experience proves to be positive or negative?	

3. How are we collaborating as a staff to ensure three-way reporting is successful for us?
 	
  ✐ Have we taken time to discuss concerns, and have we developed strategies for dealing with them?
  ✐ Have we shared ideas for a newsletter to inform parents about the three-way conference process and the three-way report?
  ✐ Have we developed a contingency plan for those parents who are unwilling or unable to participate?
  ✐ Have we arranged for conference times that work for parents, students, and teachers?
  ✐ How are we, as a staff, welcoming parents to the three-way conference (for example, having them meet for tea in the library, posting signs, providing a babysitting service for other siblings)?	

4. How am I preparing myself for three-way reporting?
 	
  ✐ What tasks have I given up so that I have the time and energy for this process?
  ✐ What are the things that I need more time to talk with my colleagues about?
  ✐ Have I prepared a guide for the conference that will help me take useful notes for the three-way report and be sure that all the important points are discussed?	

                                                           Continued next page

TEACHER CONSIDERATIONS	RESPONSE
✎ What are my major concerns about preparing the three-way reports? Are there any solutions? What am I feeling most comfortable with?	
✎ How do I set up my room so that all participants are comfortable?	
✎ Can I articulate why collaboration among students, their parents, and teachers is important in the process of student learning?	

THREE-WAY REPORTING—TOGETHER IS BETTER

TOGETHER IS BETTER when the way we report includes parents, students, and students, and teachers as valued contributors. Communication is improved when everyone has the opportunity to take part, ask for clarification, see specific examples, and know that they've been heard. In the following chapters, you will learn more about the three-way reporting process that leads to three-way reports.

NOTE: In this photo two teachers who share the class are part of the conference.

The Three-Way Reporting Process Unfolds

2

Three-Way Conferences

Until recently, most conferences involved only parents and teachers, and usually came only after report card distribution. We are suggesting that three-way conferences, each involving the teacher, parents, and student, take place, and that the written report—a three-way report—be sent home only after this conference has taken place. Teachers who choose to involve their students as active participants in three-way conferencing are finding that children know a great deal about their own learning and are key informants in the reporting process.

During three-way conferences, when students, their parents, and teachers meet to discuss their children's learning, everyone has a role to play. The children demonstrate what they know as they share their accomplishments and set new learning goals. The parents find out about their children's learning, have the opportunity to ask questions and express their ideas, and help make plans to support their children's learning at home. Teachers facilitate the three-way conversations. They support the learners *and* the parents by clarifying, elaborating, and responding to specific questions and concerns.

A SNAPSHOT OF THE THREE-WAY CONFERENCING PROCESS

1. The teacher and students prepare for the upcoming conferences. This includes building rapport with parents, sharing evidence of learning, and sharing students' reflections about their work.

2. The teacher helps parents prepare for the conference by sending home letters that outline the conference format. (See figure 3, page 32.)

3. Before each conference, the student and parents spend time reviewing the child's collection of work and viewing the different learning areas in the classroom.

4. The student, parents, and teacher then meet in the classroom conference area. The student leads the discussion about what he or she has learned, what areas he or she needs to improve upon, and what his or her learning goals are for the upcoming term.

5. Learning goals, proposed by the student in cooperation with his or her teacher, are agreed upon. The child states what he or she is going to do to achieve each goal, and both the teacher and parents commit to providing specific support.

6. The teacher keeps a record of the discussion during the conference and ensures that the conference runs smoothly by helping the student address all the relevant issues and by helping to answer parent questions.

left see figure 6, p. 36
below see figure 3, p. 32
below left see figure 1, p.9

THREE-WAY CONFERENCE GUIDE FOR TEACHERS

Student's name _____ Date _____

Areas of strength	Areas needing improvement
Notes for the conference	Additional notes

Action Plan
Goal:

Student will...	Teacher will...	Parent will...

Other notes:

Dear Parent(s):

This is what you can expect when you attend the three-way parent(s)/teacher/child conference on _____ at _____.

* You and your child will have time to look over his or her collection of work and the classroom displays and learning centers.

* You and your child will then meet with me to discuss your child's strengths, any concerns, and set new learning goals for the upcoming term.

* Your child is prepared to take an active part. There will be opportunities for you to ask questions, make comments, or express concerns.

* The parents' group has arranged to have tea and coffee available in the library for your enjoyment following the conference.

* If you have any issues you wish to discuss privately with me following the three-way conference, a sign-up sheet is available on the table to the left of the door.

* The grade 7 Buddy Program is providing a child-minding service in Mrs. Jones's room (117).

We believe that a three-way conference is one important way to support student learning. We look forward to meeting with you.

Sincerely,

Teacher

ACTION PLAN
's Goals for Upcoming Term

Action to be taken by
* **Student**

* **Parent(s)**

* **Teacher**

A TYPICAL THREE-WAY CONFERENCE — MACKENZIE'S STORY

Mackenzie and his mother, Mrs. D., arrive at the door of the classroom at 10:30 in the morning. Mackenzie's mother is holding the sheet sent by the school describing the conference. (See page 32.) A student-made sign on the door says, "Come in—Welcome!" Mr. G., the teacher, is having a conference at one end of the room with another family.

Mackenzie (grabbing his mother's hand): "Mom, come over here. I've got some stuff to show you."

Mackenzie obviously knows what is expected of him. He gets his notebooks and a folder from his work space. He pulls out a green sheet of paper entitled, "Three-Way Conference Guide for Students." (See figure 7, page 37.)

Mrs. D.: "What is all this stuff, Mackenzie?"

Mackenzie: "Oh, we got all this ready last week. Mr. G. helped."

Mackenzie turns to his pile and pulls out his folder showing his drafts of a story called "The Eagle's Adventure." He continues by showing his math book, explaining that the class is working on multiplying with two-digit numbers. He then takes his mom to look at his group-project mural and at his artwork displayed throughout the room. Mr. G. comes over and joins Mackenzie and his mom.

Mr. G.: "Did you show your mother the work you've been doing on observing and recording the growth of our bean plants?"

Mackenzie: "No, not yet."

Mr. G.: "Maybe you can show her afterwards. We should sit down now so we get time to talk."

Mackenzie, his mother, and Mr. G. sit around a table at the far end of the room. Mr. G. looks at the clock and sees that it's 10:40.

Mr. G.: "We'll be able to talk together for ten minutes, and then Mackenzie can show you anything else that he wants to."

Even though a letter has gone home prior to the conference, Mr. G. takes time to give the outline for the conference.

Mr. G.: "We've got three things to do: talk about Mackenzie's strengths, discuss any areas of concern, and agree on some specific goals for next term. I'll keep a record of the key points of this conversation and send home the summary report in a week or so. If you find you need to meet

with me again I'd be happy to do so. There's a sign-up list by the door for anyone wanting an additional conference."

Mr. G. (turning to Mackenzie): "Mackenzie, what do you do in school that you feel really good about?"

Mackenzie tells about his accomplishments and his successes. Mr. G. invites Mackenzie's mom to contribute any ideas she would like to add.

Mrs. D. (with a smile): "I noticed how organized your work space is, Mackenzie. We'll have to try to keep your room this well organized. I'm also really pleased that you have begun to read every night before going to sleep. Mr. G., thanks for letting Mackenzie bring home so many books."

Mr. G.: "You're welcome. Mackenzie and I talked about his strengths and some of the things he might choose as goals. I agree with all these strengths. One thing I would like to add is how dependable you are, Mackenzie. I can always count on you to do what you're asked to do. Mackenzie, is there anything that you feel you need to work on?"

Mackenzie: "Yes, I want to read some harder books and I want to learn how to write [handwriting]."

Mr. G.: "I am really pleased with the work you are doing. You have learned a lot this term, and I know you have worked hard. Those are reasonable goals for you. Your mother might have some ideas too. Do you have anything to add, Mrs. D.?"

Mrs. D.: "I'm worried that Mackenzie never brings any work home."

Mr. G. takes a few minutes to explain the homework policy of the school that discourages homework for children of this age because…

Mrs. D.: "That's good to know. The other thing I'd like to say is that I can see that Mackenzie is learning a lot and is happy at school. Is there anything else I need to know about? Should I be worried about anything?"

Mr. G.: "The only concern I have is that Mackenzie almost always selects non-fiction reading materials. He might like to try some fiction. One book he might start with is *Hank the Cow Dog* by John R. Erickson."

The concluding conference activity was to agree on no more than two goals for next term. Both Mackenzie's mother and Mr. G. specified what they would be willing to do to help Mackenzie achieve his goals. Mr. G. then thanked Mackenzie and his mother. He suggested that Mackenzie show her the class bean project, reminded them that there was coffee and juice available in the school library, and then excused himself to go over the conference notes (see figure 6, page 36) and prepare for the next conference.

THREE-WAY CONFERENCING—TEACHER-PROVEN IDEAS

The following pages outline some of the things that teachers have done to make three-way conferences a positive learning experience for everyone.

Idea! Playing with Possibilities   31
Idea! Helping Parents Prepare for the Conference   32
Idea! Working Out the Wrinkles   33
Idea! Providing a Safe Audience   35
Idea! Providing a Conference Guide for Teachers   36
Idea! Providing a Conference Guide for Students   37
Idea! Setting Student Goals   38
Idea! Going Further with Goal Setting   39
Idea! Reflecting on Three-Way Conferencing   40
Idea! Inviting Feedback   41

PLAYING WITH POSSIBILITIES

To help parents understand how three-way conferences might work, one staff had fun role-playing conference possibilities at a parent meeting. The staff were careful not to mock anyone through their role-play, which was videotaped so that it could be sent home to any parents unable to attend. They prepared sample materials for the role-play.

You are Jason.
- You are 6 years old.
- You are quiet, you want to please the teacher, and you are tired of being chased by girls at recess.
- You like to read and to be read to.

You are the teacher.
- You are pleased that Jason is starting to talk about his ideas in class, although he is still very quiet. He loves math.
- Your big concern is that Jason really does not like to try anything that is new.

You are Jason's dad.
- You work for a computer company.
- You are not happy about being at this interview, but your wife is at home with two sick children.
- You are concerned about Jason's spelling and the appearance of his work worries you. You want to know if everything is okay.

Figure 2   Role Cards

> *IDEA!*
>
> *HELPING PARENTS PREPARE FOR THE CONFERENCE*
>
> One teacher, realizing that parents had never experienced three-way conferencing, sent home the following letter with her students to prepare parents for their three-way conferences. The principal also sent home a letter to every parent that served to validate the process and to let parents know that every teacher was participating.

Dear Parent(s):

This is what you can expect when you attend the three-way parent(s)/teacher/child conference on _____
at _____.

- You and your child will have time to look over his or her collection of work and the classroom displays and learning centers.

- You and your child will then meet with me to discuss your child's strengths, any concerns, and set new learning goals for the upcoming term.

- Your child is prepared to take an active part. There will be opportunities for you to ask questions, make comments, or express concerns.

- The parents' group has arranged to have tea and coffee available in the library for your enjoyment following the conference.

- If you have any issues you wish to discuss privately with me following the three-way conference, a sign-up sheet is available on the table to the left of the door.

- The grade 7 Buddy Program is providing a child-minding service in Mrs. Jones's room (117).

We believe that a three-way conference is one important way to support student learning. We look forward to meeting with you.

Sincerely,

Teacher

Figure 3   Letter to Parents

IDEA!

WORKING OUT THE WRINKLES

Before starting three-way conferences, the staff in one school brainstormed all the possible wrinkles that might occur. Then they worked together to generate possible solutions.

WRINKLES	SMOOTHERS
Parents don't want their child present when they meet with the teacher.	Provide a sign-up sheet for a two-way (parent/teacher) conference.
Parent is highly critical of child, and conference focus is being lost.	Stop the direction of conversation by saying, "I need to interrupt you and remind you that the purpose of this conference is to focus on your child's strengths, look at concerns in a constructive manner, and set goals. This was all outlined in my letter to you. It appears that you have some issues outside this focus that you wish to discuss, and I'd be pleased to set another time to meet with you privately. In the meantime, I'd like to continue. Would that be possible?" (If parent is unable to cooperate, stop the conference.)
Parents don't speak English.	If the child isn't able to translate for his or her parent or doesn't feel comfortable translating, contact community groups, parents' associations, or school-board office to arrange for someone who can act as a translator.
Specialist teachers feel left out (e.g. Music, French, Physical Education).	Possibilities: • a special conference day • a separate sign-up sheet • a "drop-in center" on conference day

This page may be reproduced for teacher use.

Figure 4
Wrinkles and Smoothers

Continued next page

WRINKLES	SMOOTHERS
Learning assistance teacher wants to be involved.	Arrange four-way conferences.
Parents attack teacher's methods or style.	Brainstorm phrases to use if this situation occurs. (e.g., "I can see that you are really concerned about this. Right now, since Jeremy is here, why don't we continue Jeremy's conference and schedule a private interview to discuss your concerns.")
Parents bring siblings.	Provide a child-minding area, using para-professionals, volunteer parents, or older students to help.
Child gets silly or misbehaves (out of character).	If parent doesn't intervene, try a comment such as, "_____, this isn't like you. You must be feeling nervous. This is your time to tell your parents about your learning. We've prepared for this. Give it a try by starting with _____."
The student is enthusiastic about having a three-way conference but the parents are unavailable.	Possibilities: • Get parents' permission to have older brother, sister, aunt, last year's teacher, older buddy, or school counsellor attend. (A report written by the teacher will be sent home.)

Figure 4
Wrinkles and Smoothers (cont'd.)

IDEA!

PROVIDING A SAFE AUDIENCE

One teacher had older student buddies help their young buddies rehearse the review of their collections of work. The teacher provided the big buddies with response sheets, which they filled in at the end of the practice conferences.

Dear Buddy
  I really liked

☆ _____

☆ _____
  Be sure to show your
parents _____

_____

_____

_____

Signed _____
      (older buddy)

Figure 5 Response Sheet—
Younger Buddy/Older Buddy

IDEA!

PROVIDING A CONFERENCE GUIDE FOR TEACHERS

One school found it useful to develop conference guides for the teachers. Before the conferences, these guides were used for preparation notes. During the conferences, the teachers used them to record notes in all areas. Following the three-way conferences, these sheets became the frames for the three-way reports.

THREE-WAY CONFERENCE GUIDE FOR TEACHERS

Student's name _____   Date _____

Areas of strength	Areas needing improvement
Notes for the conference	Additional notes

Action Plan
Goal:

Student will...	Teacher will...	Parent will...

Other notes:

Figure 6
Conference Guide for Teachers

Blackline master in Appendix C.

(IDEA!)

PROVIDING A CONFERENCE GUIDE FOR STUDENTS

Teachers found that providing students with an open-ended frame helped them feel confident and prepared for the conference.

THREE-WAY CONFERENCE GUIDE FOR STUDENTS

Name _____   Date _____

Things I'm really good at

Two things I need to improve…

Things to show…

My next term goal is…

Figure 7
Conference Guide for Students
Blackline master in Appendix C.

SETTING STUDENT GOALS

As new learning goals are set at the end of each three-way conference, one teacher worked with her students to practise setting goals in anticipation of the conference. To help students understand what a goal is, she worked with the class as a whole to answer the question: "What things could we improve as a class?"

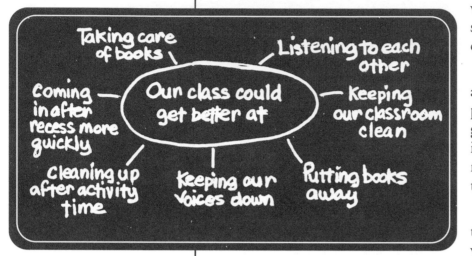

After they had brainstormed a list of possibilities, students printed their initials beside the goal that they thought was most important to them. The goal that received the most initials became the class goal for the week.

A second list describing what they could do to reach their goal was developed by the group. At the end of the week the students made a third list, one that recorded their progress and accomplishments towards their goal. The final step was to determine whether they wanted to reset the goal for another week or whether they could go on to a new goal.

CLASS RECORD SHEET		
The goal	Evidence of meeting the goal	Resetting the goal
Taking care of books	At the end of the day all the books will be on the bookshelf with their spines facing out. Whenever someone sees a book left out they will put it away.	We did it! Our next goal is...

Figure 8   Class Record Sheet
Blackline master in Appendix C.

(*IDEA!*)

GOING FURTHER WITH GOAL SETTING

After lots of practice setting and resetting goals as a class, one teacher helped students prepare their individual goals in anticipation of their upcoming three-way conferences. They met as a group and shared all the goals that they felt were important. Each student then selected the goal that he or she felt was most important for him or her. These were recorded in their conference guides by the teacher so that they would have them ready to share during their conferences.

Figure 9
Goal-Setting Frame for Students

My goal is ___to come in after recess when the other kids do___

_____ because ___my class is waiting for me and they want to go to the gym___

ACTION PLAN
Colby   's Goals for Upcoming Term
1. to come in after recess when the other children do
2. to be a more considerate group member

Action to be taken by

• **Student**   I will listen and not flick stuff

• **Parent(s)**   I will try some of these same ideas at home (e.g. at dinner time)

• **Teacher**   I will make sure the group time is not too long and will give Colby positive feedback

see figure 1, p.9

REFLECTING ON THREE-WAY CONFERENCING

Some students were really worried about participating in the three-way conferences. Their teacher spent time talking with the students about their feelings. At the end of their discussion, they wrote in their journals for ten minutes. Following the conferences, the students talked about what had taken place, then spent another ten minutes recording in their journals how they each felt about their own three-way conference.

One staff met after their three-way conferences to share successes and concerns. One group shared the following advice with other members of the staff.

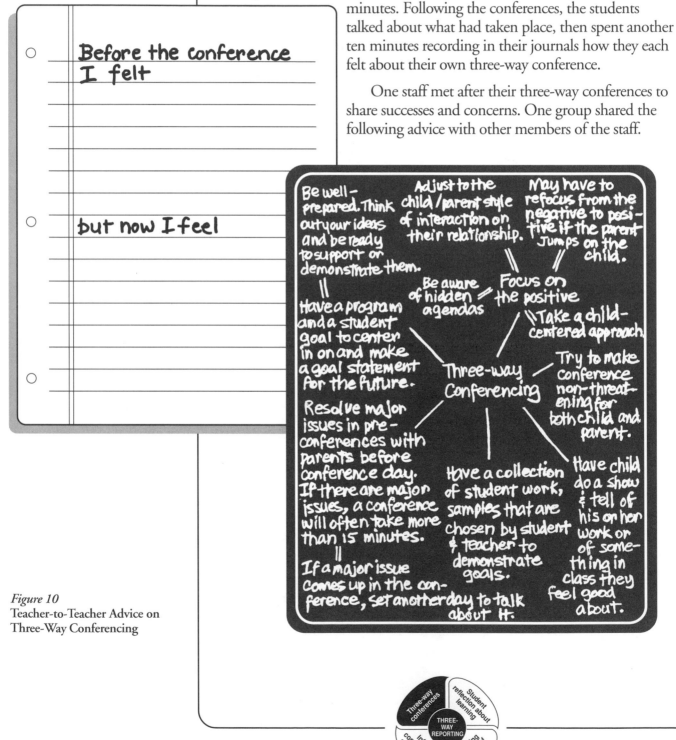

Figure 10
Teacher-to-Teacher Advice on Three-Way Conferencing

IDEA!

INVITING FEEDBACK

One teacher, wanting to invite feedback from his students' parents about their recent conferences, sent home a response form. Another school sent each parent a similar response form that accompanied their child's three-way report. The school provided a box in the office to collect responses, as some parents indicated that they were more comfortable responding to the process anonymously.

PARENT RESPONSE TO CONFERENCE

What we liked about the conference: _____

_____

_____

_____

_____

What we need to know more about: _____

_____

_____

_____

_____

Two suggestions for the next conference: _____

_____

_____

_____

_____

Other comments? _____

_____

_____

_____

_____

_____

_____

_____

_____

_____

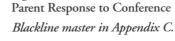

Figure 11
Parent Response to Conference
Blackline master in Appendix C.

LEARNING FROM LISTENING

As we listen to the comments of students, parents, and teachers, we continue to learn more about the process.

Parent: "If I could be given some idea before the conference how my child was doing, I could be prepared with questions or concerns."

Parent: "Parents should know the teacher's concerns before the three-way conference with the child takes place. Then the parent would have more time to think about solving any problems before they met with both the teacher and their child."

Informal communication is a crucial component of the reporting process. There should be no surprises when it comes to evaluation. Parents need to know the agenda.

Parent: "I like the fact that my child is very involved and thus feels more responsible for her own schoolwork. It also makes her feel proud of her accomplishments."

We wonder why we have waited so long to include children in the process.

Parent: "I believe that my child's social development is as significant as her intellectual development, but I was hesitant to confront the teachers with questions about this important area."

Providing the opportunity for a follow-up parent-teacher conference (without the child in attendance) is also important. Though only a small percentage of parents will take advantage of the opportunity, they need to know they have this option. In some cases, these conferences will be suggested by the teacher.

Teacher: "Before we began three-way conferencing, when I had to do all the talking and showing at parent-teacher conferences, I could hardly walk at the end of the day. I was always exhausted."

The role of teachers is changing. We believe that involving others enhances student learning—we cannot accomplish as much working alone.

Learning Assistance Teacher: "That was the first time we all sat down together and listened to what the student was capable of doing and what he hoped to achieve. I know his teacher and I will work together more effectively now."

It is important to make an effort to involve everyone who works with the child in the conference. It may need to be a four-way conference for some children.

Teacher: "One conference was awful—why is that the one that I remember over all the others, which were great?"

As teachers, we need to focus on our successes while learning from our mistakes. We forget that we are also learners in this process, and that learners learn through trial and re-trial.

Teacher: "I was really pleased by how well Raul translated for his parents. It just didn't seem to be a problem."

Our students are very capable of helping us communicate with their parents. We need to ask them for help and for advice regarding what is appropriate in their culture.

Student: "I didn't know what my mom would say when she saw my collection of work. But Mom smiled and said she loved it. I felt good."

New communication about learning between parents and their children can be initiated by three-way conferencing.

THREE-WAY CONFERENCING—KEEPING FOCUSED

TEACHER CONSIDERATIONS	RESPONSE

1. How have I involved the students in the process of three-way conferencing?
   - Do students have their own notes—a guide—to help them remember everything?
   - Have there been opportunities for rehearsal with peers?
   - Have students had a chance to talk about this process and express feelings?
   - How am I incorporating student input into the three-way conferencing?
   - Have they had time and support to prepare their collections of work for parent viewing?

2. How have I involved the parents in the process of three-way conferencing?
   - Have we talked about what happens during a three-way conference, or have I sent home materials to help them prepare themselves?
   - How have I helped parents prepare their questions and suggestions?
   - How have I invited parent response?
   - If parents have made suggestions, have I considered how I can ensure that their needs are better met?

3. How are we collaborating as a staff?
   - Have we talked about the role of specialist teachers (music, French, learning assistance) and arranged how they will be involved?
   - Have we taken time to discuss issues of concern to us? Have we brainstormed solutions?
   - Have we shared ideas for a newsletter informing parents about the three-way conference process and three-way reporting?
   - Have we developed a contingency plan for parents who are unwilling or unable to participate?
   - Have we coordinated conference times that work for parents, students, and teachers?
   - How are we, as a staff, welcoming parents to the three-way conference (for example, by making tea available in the library, posting signs, providing supervision for siblings, sharing student-made videos of the school at work)?

     Continued next page

TEACHER CONSIDERATIONS	RESPONSE
4. How am I preparing myself for three-way conferencing?	

4. How am I preparing myself for three-way conferencing?
- ✎ What have I given up doing so that I have the time to take on this process?
- ✎ What are the things that I need more time to talk about with my colleagues or with parents before I go any further with three-way conferencing?
- ✎ Have I prepared a guide for each conference that will help me take notes for the three-way report and be sure all the important points are discussed for each child?
- ✎ What is my major concern? What am I feeling most comfortable with?
- ✎ How do I set up my room so that all participants are comfortable?
- ✎ Can I articulate why three-way conferencing is important in the process of student learning?

THREE-WAY CONFERENCING—TOGETHER IS BETTER

TOGETHER IS BETTER when teachers see the parents with their children, and the parents see their children with the teacher. Everyone observes and is informed by the interaction between and among all participants. The children have the most significant adults in their lives showing interest in their learning and making commitments to support them.

3

Informal Communication

Teachers can use a variety of ways to communicate informally with parents about their children's learning including

- having after-school conversations
- sending notes home
- making telephone calls
- having students take their work collections home to share with their parents
- inviting parents to tell teachers what they think of their child's work
- using "back and forth" books in which children record what has been done at school that day and inviting parent response
- developing a sign-out video that shows snippets of classroom activities

Informal conversations between teachers and parents, either at school or by phone, often help develop the rapport necessary for open communication in subsequent meetings. Having children select and take home evidence of their own learning is one way of helping parents further their understanding of what goes on in schools. The informal sharing of student samples at various times during the school year provides a starting place for conversations between parents and their children. Inviting parents to record what they think of their children's work acknowledges that parents' comments are important for both the children and the teacher.

A SNAPSHOT OF INFORMAL
COMMUNICATION: A PAGE FROM THE ALBUM

There is no one way to develop rapport with parents. Informal communication invites a range of responses—from teachers, from parents, and from students. Here are three different snapshots from the album.

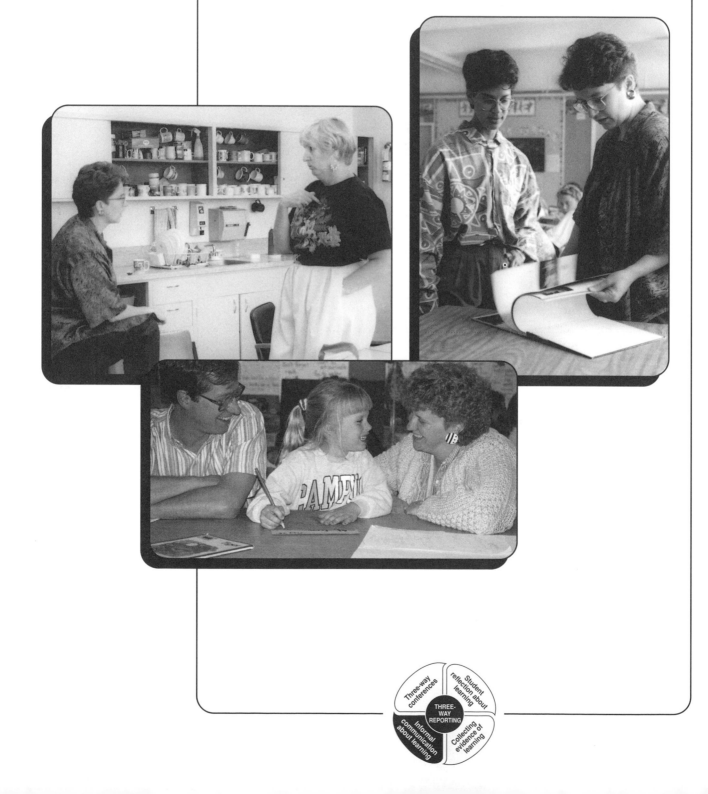

INFORMAL COMMUNICATION—TEACHER-PROVEN IDEAS

The following examples of informal communications have proved successful for parents, students, and teachers alike.

Idea! Capturing Student Learning   50
Idea! Viewing a Video   51
Idea! Inviting Parent Response   52
Idea! Providing Viewing Guidelines for Parents   53
Idea! Demonstrating Progress   54
Idea! Showing What We Know   55
Idea! Informal Reports to Parents   57
Idea! Making a Birthday Call   61
Idea! Getting Information from Parents   62
Idea! Giving Parents an Active Learning Experience   63

CAPTURING STUDENT LEARNING

One teacher took pictures of each child at work in the classroom, wrote a brief, two-line comment about each child, and sent these home to parents.

February 1992,

Here I am at school.

I am trying to read lots of

different books. I can read Frog

and Toad. I am writing 4 or 5
sentences every day.

Mrs. Stacy

(scribing for Mackenzie)

Figure 12
Here I am at school…

(*IDEA!*)

VIEWING A VIDEO

In one class, the teacher set up a video camera with a wide-angle lens in the corner of the classroom. At selected periods during the day, she turned the camera on and recorded her students at work at various tasks. The teacher developed a brief viewing guide and glued it on the outside of the video's carrying case. As long as they used the sign-out sheet, the video could be taken home by the students to share with their parents.

VIDEO VIEWING GUIDE

This is our class at work. We are _____

_____

_____

We also are _____

_____

Three key points I want to stress are _____

_____

_____

_____

_____

Enjoy the video!   _____
                                                  [Teacher's name]

Viewers' Responses—We invite your comments!

Comments	Signature

Figure 13
Video Viewing Guide
Blackline master in Appendix C.

THREE-WAY REPORTING

Three-way conferences

Student reflection about learning

Informal communication about learning

Collecting evidence of learning

INVITING PARENT RESPONSE

One way to encourage parents to communicate is to include a parent response sheet with collections of student work that are sent home or viewed in the class. Two examples are illustrated.

Figure 14A   Parent Response Sheet for Portfolio Review (Example 1)

PARENT RESPONSE SHEET FOR PORTFOLIO REVIEW

Comments

What two things would you like to have include

1. _____

_____

_____

_____

2. _____

_____

_____

_____

Signature(s) _____

PARENT RESPONSE SHEET FOR PORTFOLIO REVIEW

Portfolio Review

Date _____

Name _____

Two Stars

★

★

One Wish

Figure 14B   Parent Response Sheet for Portfolio Review (Example 2)

Blackline masters in Appendix C.

IDEA!

PROVIDING VIEWING GUIDELINES FOR PARENTS

Many teachers found that parents got more out of viewing their children's work when they were given a viewing guide or suggestions about what to look for in the work.

Dear Parent(s)—

Nothing succeeds like success. When we know we have done something right, we feel good about ourselves, we accept challenges more readily and enthusiastically, and learning becomes easier. As you look through these pages, look for your child's successes. Compliment your child on the detail of his or her book reports, the imaginative drawing used to represent a book he or she has read, the enjoyment he or she finds in learning center activities. Let his or her written comments be your guide.

After listening to your compliments, your child will be ready to listen to your wishes. Be selective about wishes for improvement. Giving too many wishes may do more damage than good. Pick out one or two areas that are important and that you feel your child is capable of improving. As a rule of thumb, we suggest two compliments before one wish.

Enjoy!

_____
[Teacher's name]

(Letter thanks to Peter Gallie, School District #62, British Columbia.)

Figure 15 Portfolio Viewing
Guidelines for Parents

DEMONSTRATING PROGRESS

Many teachers reported that the work samples parents most appreciated were ones that showed progress.

BEFORE	NOW
[Early example of child's work.]	[Later example of child's work.]
At first, I	but now I

Figure 16 "Then and Now" Look at Students' Work

IDEA!

SHOWING WHAT WE KNOW

Many teachers are designing ways to share what their students can do. As evaluation is ongoing, informal reports are one way that teachers can share information more frequently with parents. There are a number of key elements to successful informal reports: there should be some student involvement in their preparation; they should show progress over time; they should include a place for parents to respond to children's work; and they should not take too much class time to prepare. These reports are often sent home prior to a three-way conference to update the parents' information about their children's learning.

Step-by-step process of developing an informal report:

1. Each child selects something he or she has done in class; for example, a story, a drawing, a sample of problem solving, selections from a novel. Teachers may choose to provide the criteria for selection and be involved in the selection. They may ask children to select pieces of their work that show how they used to write and how they write now, how they used to spell and how they spell now, how they used to read and how they read now, or something that they used to find difficult and now find easy to do. Teachers may ask children to produce something special for the informal report or to explain to parents what they have been learning.

2. Each student explains why he or she has selected that particular example of work. Sometimes teachers choose to respond to the child's explanation.

Month ___Shaun March___

There were ___102___

___Jelly Beans___ in the jar.

These people had close guesses:

~~Shaun~~ me 97

___ 16y 115

___inder 112

___addy 93

Number Sheet

I Choose This^ because I New It was close Number!

Three-way conferences · Student reflection about learning · THREE-WAY REPORTING · Informal communication about learning · Collecting evidence of learning

3. The work is shared with parents, and students invite their parents to respond. The response is framed in such as way as to ensure the message is directed to the child.

Figure 17A   Parent Response to Student Work (Example 1)

Blackline master in Appendix C.

Dear _____Ricky_____
[Student's name]

In looking at your work so far, I/we would like to compliment you on

your French and spelling. They have improved a lot.

The most important thing I/we would like to say to you now is

You are trying hard in math. You made a really good effort on your Sun report.

As your parent(s), I/we _____are proud of your work so far. Keep it up!_

_____Mom_____
[Parent's signature]

_____Dad_____
[Parent's signature]

P.S. Dear _____Mr. Johnson_____
[Teacher's name]

I/we would like to let you know that _____we were wondering about Ricky's attitude and class involvement._

At school I like . . .

w'iting

Dear _____Franny_____

I was pleased to notice _how well you are doing in math, and that you are doing so much printing. I also liked the happy picture on the front cover._

At the conference with you and your teacher I would like to know more about _how happy and confident you seem at school and if you are getting along well with the other kids. Do you want any extra help from Dad and me at home?_

M. Alvarez
[Parent's signature]

Figure 17B   Parent Response to Student Work (Example 2)

IDEA!

INFORMAL REPORTS TO PARENTS

Informal reports portray the work that students have been doing in school and, as such, are unique to each student. Here are examples of informal reports that teachers have helped students prepare to take home to parents.

__Kenzie__
my name

What can I do?

reading	I can reading Frog and Toad
writing	I can writ abied the sun. the sun is nos
math	I like math. math is fun. I can mickocwishins.

Figure 18A   Informal Report to Parents (Example 1)

(Side 1)

MY INFORMAL REPORT TO MY PARENT(S)

Date _____   Name _____

1. The most important thing in our classroom that I am trying to do well is _____
_____
_____

2. This is important to me because _____
_____
_____

3. Two things that I have done well this term are _____
_____
_____

4. One thing that I need to work harder at is ____
_____
_____

5. Something that I am proud about this term is __
_____
_____

6. My goal(s) for next term is (are) _____
_____
_____

7. Attached are some samples of my work. Please __
_____
_____

_____

(Side 2)

PARENT'S RESPONSE

1. _____ , I compliment you on your work sample. I especially liked
_____
_____
_____

2. One thing I would like you to work on is _____
_____
_____
_____

3. During our three-way conference in November I would like to know more about
_____
_____
_____

_____
[Parent's signature]

Figure 18B Informal Report to
Parents (Example 2)
Blackline masters in Appendix C.

THREE-WAY
REPORTING

Three-way conferences

Student reflection about learning

Informal communication about learning

Collecting evidence of learning

Informal Report   by Terry

I've been learning about

adding
Printing
Math
calendar
Writing
soccer
Salmon
P.E
Swimming
Big Books
Library Research
Reading
Art
Home Reading Program
Cooperating
Music
clean-up
class meeting
Special person of the week

I want to work on writing harder words

This is what I am thinking about working on for next term

Parents Response

I would like to compliment you on: the long story you wrote and the big words you used. I also was pleased to see how neat your printing is.

Terry, during the conference I would like to talk with you more about what you do in gym and how you figure out words you don't know in reading. We are looking forward to hearing about all the neat things you do in class. ___L. Mason___

[Parent's signature]

Figure 18C   Informal Report to Parents (Example 3)

THREE-WAY REPORTING — Three-way conferences / Student reflection about learning / Collecting evidence of learning / Informal communication about learning

All about __Emily__
Age: __7½__ Date: __Oct 25, 1991__

Teachers: __Mrs. Davidson__
__Mrs. Politano__

I am proud of __my Writing, my friends,__
__and how I get along__
__with people__

My goals are __my reading to get better.__
__—at reading to sing more__

My teacher(s) would like to say __how impressed we__
__are with Emily's work in drama.__
__She creates imaginative stories and__
__encourages other classmates to do the same.__

Parent's Comments: __Emily is really happy at school.__
__Plays are her very favorite activity.__

Figure 18D Informal Report
to Parents (Example 4)

Blackline master in Appendix C.

IDEA!

MAKING A BIRTHDAY CALL

Many teachers make it a practice to call parents throughout the year to share some positive and pleasant information. One teacher calls children on the morning of their birthday to wish them Happy Birthday. She uses this opportunity to tell the parents one or two things that she appreciates about their child.

Birthdays

September ~
10 Jamie   555-6503
12 Lucie   555-0296

October ~
3 Martina   555-1345
17 Stefan   555-9618
24 Kwan   555-1702

November ~
9 Amelie
12 Raj

December ~
1 Mikhail
19 Edward
28 Milan

January ~
7 Andrew
29 Maria
31 Courtney

February ~
2 Yasmin
15 Gregory

March ~
21 Elizabeth
29 Angel

April ~
8 Matt
26 Salvatore
28 Jonathon

May ~
3 Anita
12 Louisa
13 Thuan
22 Sangeeta

June ~
3 Baillie
20 Megan

July ~
4 Ludmila
7 Ashad

August ~
19 Lupe
25 Jessica

THREE-WAY REPORTING
- Three-way conferences
- Student reflection about learning
- Collecting evidence of learning
- Informal communication about learning

> ## IDEA!
>
> ### GETTING INFORMATION FROM PARENTS
>
> One teacher finds it helpful to begin the school year by asking parents to share their knowledge of their child.

Language Arts
INFORMATION SHEET

Prior to finalizing my long-range plans for this year, I would appreciate information from you regarding your child's perceived strengths and needs.

As parent(s) you are in the best position to evaluate your child's use of language and language skills (such as reading and writing) in "the real world." I would appreciate your consideration of the following questions and your careful appraisal of your child's skills.

Thank you!

_____
[Teacher's signature]

✐ We/I would like our child to learn _____
this year. We/I would like our child to be exposed to _____
and _____ .

_____ is particularly good at _____ and _____ .
He/she is also able to _____ easily. However, in spite of
_____ 's talents, _____ needs lots of assistance to _____
and_____ .

✐ In general, a perfect Language Arts program for _____ would _____
_____
_____ .

✐ If you ever want _____ 's undivided attention you just have to mention
_____ or _____ . But whatever
you do, don't ever mention _____ !!

Good luck in your endeavors!!   Sincerely,

_____

_____ 's parent(s)

Figure 19
Information from Parents

Blackline master in Appendix C

(IDEA!)

GIVING PARENTS AN ACTIVE LEARNING EXPERIENCE

To make parents' night more informative, some teachers came up with a plan that included children and gave parents the opportunity to gain information about the classroom program and to ask questions.

One evening, parents were invited to help their children make cloth covers for their soon-to-be-published books. When the covers were made, the children had an opportunity to show their book drafts to their parents. The teacher then gave a brief overview (about 15 minutes long) of the steps involved in the writing process.

Other possibilities for parents' night include having parents take an active role in learning-center activities, participating in a mini-lesson, and using math manipulatives.

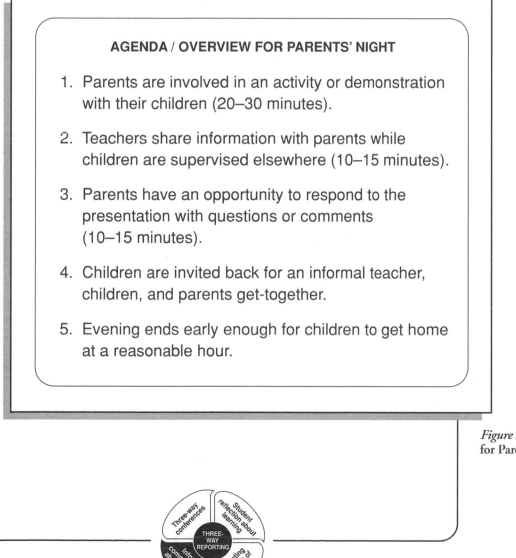

AGENDA / OVERVIEW FOR PARENTS' NIGHT

1. Parents are involved in an activity or demonstration with their children (20–30 minutes).

2. Teachers share information with parents while children are supervised elsewhere (10–15 minutes).

3. Parents have an opportunity to respond to the presentation with questions or comments (10–15 minutes).

4. Children are invited back for an informal teacher, children, and parents get-together.

5. Evening ends early enough for children to get home at a reasonable hour.

Figure 20 Agenda/Overview for Parents' Night

LEARNING FROM LISTENING

As we listen to the comments of students, parents, and teachers, we continue to learn more about the process.

Teacher: "Some parents didn't know what to say to their children about their work, while others were really negative. I learned to send home a guide sheet before the conferences so that parents would know the significance of what they were seeing."

We learned that parents need help to see exactly what learning is being demonstrated.

Parent: "It was a real treat to get a phone call and hear something positive."

We open communication with parents when we begin with children's successes.

Teacher: "I'm getting to know my students' parents better by seeing their responses to their children's work. I now know what they are concerned about."

Informal communication builds the foundation for more open communication and helps prepare us for the conferences.

Parent: "Because we had been talking and seeing what Sam could do all along, I didn't feel nervous about the interview."

The time we take to build rapport pays off in the quality of our conferences. People who know each other can have much more meaningful conversations.

Student: "I really liked taking home my portfolio. My mom just loved it, and I liked having a sheet for her to write what she liked about it."

Informal communication helps the children by giving them more opportunities to show their parents what they know and can do.

Teacher: "After I made the first birthday phone call I was really hooked on the idea because both the child and his parents were so pleased by such a small thing."

It's the small things we do that let people know we are all humans and that we care.

INFORMAL COMMUNICATION—KEEPING FOCUSED

TEACHER CONSIDERATIONS	RESPONSE
1. How have I involved the students in the process of informal communication? ✐ Do students have a variety of opportunities to share their learning with their parents? ✐ Have they had practice selecting and commenting on their own work? ✐ Have I helped to ensure that they receive supportive feedback from parents?	
2. How have I involved the parents in the process of informal communication? ✐ Have I used a variety of ways during the year to invite them to comment on their children's work? ✐ How have I helped parents make supportive comments in response to their children's work? ✐ How have I helped them "see" the learning that is developing?	
3. How are we collaborating as a staff? ✐ Have we taken time for discussions about possible ways and formats for informal communication? ✐ Have we shared ways to communicate with both parents if they are living apart? ✐ Have we found ways of being consistent as a staff in keeping parents informed? ✐ Have we, as a staff, talked about our shared expectations of students and their learning?	
4. How am I preparing myself for informal communication with parents? ✐ What have I given up doing so that I have time to take on this process? ✐ What is my major concern? What am I feeling most comfortable with? ✐ How do I ensure that I have contacted all my students' parents and that there will be no unhappy surprises when it comes to the three-way conferences and the reports? ✐ Can I articulate why informal communication is important in the process of student learning?	

INFORMAL COMMUNICATION—TOGETHER IS BETTER

TOGETHER IS BETTER: When communication occurs between teachers and parents, everyone learns more about children as learners; further, children come to realize that everyone is coming together to support them.

Evidence of Learning

Everything that occurs in a classroom is potential evidence of student learning. Evidence consists of observations of children at work, the products they create, and what they communicate in the conversations we have with them about their learning.

Evidence of learning is
- a student's journal
- a student working with another student in the classroom
- two students demonstrating a science project for a small group
- a group of students presenting a choral reading
- a student telling what he knows about the number five

Evidence is used to demonstrate the learning that is taking place in the classroom. Involving students in the collection of this evidence helps them develop a sense of ownership and responsibility for their own learning. Inviting parents to provide evidence of their children's learning gets them thinking more about their children as learners.

observations of children at work

the products children create

what children say in our conversations about learning

A SNAPSHOT OF "EVIDENCE OF LEARNING"

1. Talk with the students about the purpose of collecting evidence.

2. Set aside class time for students to make selections from the work that they have produced.

3. Work with students to establish criteria for their selection.

4. Involve students in talking about who they will be showing their collections of work to and determining the most useful way to display their work.

5. Include a sheet that invites those who look at the student's collection of work to respond.

below   see figure 28, p. 78
right   see figure 29, p. 79

An effective project includes...

- a title page ☐
- a Table of Contents ☐
- interesting facts ☐
- a list of books, magazine and journals read
- headings that "tell" about the section ☐
- names of those interview
- pictures that help the reader understand ☐
- films and TV programs watched

You can see I know this because...

When I chose to include this example of my writing in my portfolio I remembered that...

Fiction
- has a good story
- uses interesting language
- has a beginning, a middle, and an end
- uses a variety of sentences, both simple and complex

Non-fiction
- gives information
- groups information under main headings
- has a table of contents
- has diagrams or pictures to give additional information

I also know that it is important that my work is neat and that it has been edited for spelling and sentence structure.

The piece of work I have chosen is...

It shows...

I want you to notice...

Please give me one compliment and ask me one question after you read my selection.

I put this in my portfolio on _____   _____
　　　　　　　　　　　　　　　　　[date]　　　　　　[signature]

THREE-WAY REPORTING

Three-way conferences
Student reflection about learning
Informal communication about learning
Collecting evidence of learning

EVIDENCE OF LEARNING—TEACHER-PROVEN IDEAS

Some colleagues have described the following ways of collecting evidence as successful for them.

Idea! Showing Your Knowledge   70
Idea! Brainstorming Evidence of Learning   71
Idea! Recording Activities Done at Learning Centers   72
Idea! Constructing a Whole-Class Question-and-Answer Grid   73
Idea! Thinking About Writing   74
Idea! Setting Challenges for Finding Evidence   75
Idea! Getting Parents to Provide Evidence of Learning   76
Idea! Modeling for the Class   77
Idea! Using Criteria   78
Idea! Improving the Selection of Work for Students' Collections   79

IDEA!

SHOWING YOUR KNOWLEDGE

In one classroom, the students showed their parents evidence of what they were learning by filling out and taking home a letter.

Dear   Mom and Dad

You may know that snails are slow, but did you know that
- they carry their houses with them
- they leave a gooey trail
- they can go over sharp objects without hurting themselves

I can tell you two more things about snails. Just ask me!

Love,

Jodie

Figure 21 Students Tell Their Parents What They've Learned

BRAINSTORMING EVIDENCE OF LEARNING

One teacher asked her students to brainstorm all the evidence they could think of that they were reading. She recorded this information on a piece of chart paper. When they were finished, she asked two children to record the information neatly on a piece of paper, which was then photocopied so that each child could take it home to be shared with his or her parents.

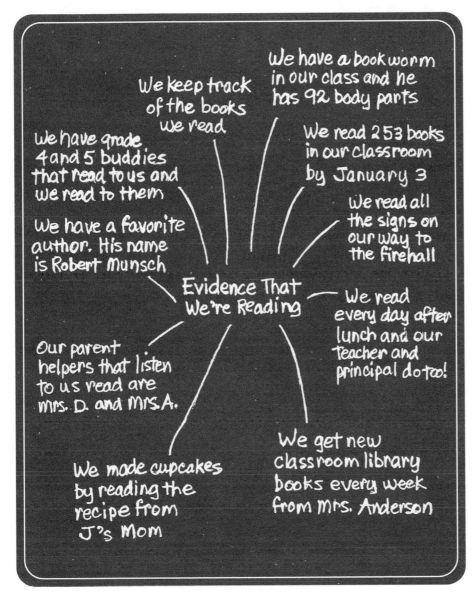

Figure 22 Brainstorm Evidence of Learning

IDEA!

RECORDING ACTIVITIES DONE AT LEARNING CENTERS

Another teacher wanted her students to keep track of which learning centers they worked at each week. At the end of each center time, they checked off in the record book the centers that they had used. At the end of each week, the teacher took two or three minutes and asked the children to turn to a partner and

- ✎ share their list
- ✎ talk about their favorite center
- ✎ tell their partner which center they hadn't tried and where they might go the following week
- ✎ explain what they would tell their parents about what they had learned at the centers

> **Name:**
> **Date:**
>
> Math Center ☐
> Reading Center ☐
> Sand Table ☐
> Water Table ☐
> Theater Center ☐
> Research Center ☐
> Science Center ☐
> Special Interest Center ☐
> Living Things Center ☐

Figure 23 Student's Record of Learning Centers Visited

IDEA!

*CONSTRUCTING A WHOLE-CLASS
QUESTION-AND-ANSWER GRID*

One teacher helped his students collect evidence of their learning during
a field trip by involving them in a pre-trip activity that involved brainstorming questions about the recycling depot they were going to visit.
The questions were recorded on a class grid, with one copy given to all
children to take with them and record their answers. When they returned,
the students provided evidence of their learning by sharing the answers.

Question: What do they do with all the glass stuff?	Question: Why don't they take plastic?	Question: Do they have to sort out different kinds of metal?
Question: Where does the stuff go?	Question: How much do they collect?	Question: Do they make lots of money?

Figure 24 Class Question-and-Answer Grid

⬭ *IDEA!*

THINKING ABOUT WRITING

One teacher had given her students many group experiences with collect-ing evidence of learning. They had selected and dated pieces to include in their writing folders. They had selected favorite pieces, circled favorite lines, selected powerful words, and created an editor's checklist. This time she asked her students to do this on their own. Each student was to select another piece of writing and fill out the following form.

One thing I like…	One thing I need to change…
One thing my parent(s) would really like about this piece…	One thing my teacher would notice about my writing is…

Figure 25
Thinking About Writing

Blackline master in Appendix C.

IDEA!

SETTING CHALLENGES FOR FINDING EVIDENCE

One teacher sets daily challenges for her children to find or show evidence of their learning/thinking. She uses the last fifteen minutes of each day to have students tell about or show evidence of

- something that they are proud of
- solving a problem
- something that they did alone
- something that they did with someone else
- something that they found hard to do
- a mistake that they realized they had made
- something that their teacher would be surprised they could do
- something that they were surprised they could do
- something that they wanted to have more time to do

"I want you to know that I remembered my goal of watching for punctuation by going over my rough draft about whales with Jamie. If you read it now you'll see that I have good punctuation."

"I'm really proud that I can play seven songs on my recorder. I've really been practicing."

"You can tell that I was really thinking when I made my computer because I used a box to add a disk drive."

GETTING PARENTS TO PROVIDE EVIDENCE OF LEARNING

One teacher invited parents to contribute evidence of their children's learning. Once the parents knew that evidence of learning at home is valued, they were delighted to provide examples as long as they were assured that the originals would be returned safely. Copies of lists, photographs, letters, maps, newspaper clippings, diagrams, and plans that children make at home enrich the child's collection of work and give insight into the child as a learner outside of school.

Sheena has recently managed to obtain her last swimming badge and now hopes to start springboard diving lessons.

Sheena completed her babysitters' training course last month. She did well on her test and has put together a kids' box to keep the children she's babysitting entertained.

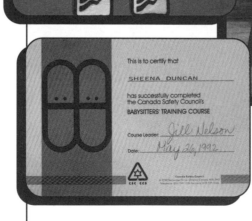

Sheena completed her Pony Club Stable Management Course last week. She is now getting ready to take her 'C' level test. Horses are still Sheena's first love.

Figure 26 Parents Provide Evidence of Learning

IDEA!

MODELING FOR THE CLASS

One teacher helps students see that evidence of learning does not have to be only test results or a check mark on a piece of paper. After observing the students during the day and making notes, he takes time to share with the whole class the evidence of learning that he had seen, thus modeling observation of evidence for the students.

"Shawn, most of the sentences in your story on whales had periods at the end. Now I know that you understand where to put periods in your writing."

"Angela, when I heard you explain to Andrew how to do the math questions, I realized that you had learned how to multiply with two numbers."

"Jake, when I asked you to tell me about the main character in the book that you were reading, you showed me how well you understood and how much you liked what you were reading."

He emphasized that evidence was found in more than work products, by giving specific examples of students demonstrating and telling what they know. Sometimes he recorded this information on the board to show different places to look for evidence of learning.

He modeled this process by using the frames illustrated, then provided frames for students to do this on their own.

This Evidence	Shows That…
When I did my map I put on a legend.	I understand how a map works.

OR

This Evidence	Shows That…
when you asked me to use one of the books I'm reading at home for reading work at school I didn't want to because it changes the way I read.	I know that sometimes reading is just for fun.

Figure 27 Frames to Help Students Identify Evidence of Learning

USING CRITERIA

One teacher, whose class does a lot of projects, involves children in setting the criteria for a successful project. The list is then photocopied and children record how their projects match the criteria. This helps the students identify what they have accomplished and provides them with some direction for goal setting.

An effective project includes...

a title page	☐		a Table of Contents	☐
interesting facts	☐		a list of books, magazines, and journals read	☐
headings that "tell" about the section	☐		names of those interviewed	☐
pictures that help the reader understand	☐		films and TV programs watched	☐

You can see I know this because...

I have everything in my folder. I showed my project to James and he checked it.

Figure 28   Using Criteria

Blackline master in Appendix C.

IDEA!

*IMPROVING THE SELECTION OF WORK
FOR STUDENTS' COLLECTIONS*

A colleague began to work with his students to collect evidence of their
work. He was helping them to select evidence that would fit specific criteria
(such as finding examples that would show perseverance, process, or improvement). As he reflected on this first experience, he found that he
needed a more "generic" record that would open up student choice and
allow for response from peers, teachers, or parents or for reflection and goal
setting. As a result the following form was developed.

**When I chose to include this example of my writing in my portfolio I
remembered that…**

Fiction
- has a good story
- uses interesting language
- has a beginning, a middle, and
  an end
- uses a variety of sentences, both
  simple and complex

Non-fiction
- gives information
- groups information under
  main headings
- has a table of contents
- has diagrams or pictures to give
  additional information

**I also know that it is important that my work is neat and that it has
been edited for spelling and sentence structure.**

The piece of work I have chosen is…

It shows…

I want you to notice…

Please give me one compliment and ask me one question after you
read my selection.

I put this in my portfolio on _____ _____
                                          [date]   [signature]

Figure 29 Improving Selection
for Students' Work Collections

Blackline master in Appendix C.

THREE-WAY REPORTING
- Three-way conferences
- Student reflection about learning
- Collecting evidence of learning
- Informal communication about learning

LEARNING FROM LISTENING

As we listen to the comments of students, parents, and teachers, we continue to learn more about the process.

Teacher: "It seems as though we can never get it right the first time. We always have to try and re-try."

We need to give ourselves permission to try and try again. Our work can never be more than a "work-in-progress."

Teacher: "We finished putting together our first collections of work, now I know what to do next time."

While we can learn some things from our colleagues' experiences, we make it our own by doing it in our own way—a way that makes sense for us and for our students and their parents.

Parent: "This scrapbook helps me get a picture of what my child does in school and what he can tell me about what he is learning."

Collections of student work are one way of bringing parents "into" classrooms. And when students can articulate what it is they are learning, parents gain confidence in what we are doing in schools; they see the proof.

Parent: "There were too many things to look at. I didn't have the time."

Less is better. Parents are busy people, and we need to be careful not to overwhelm them.

Student: "I didn't want to take my folder home."

There are so many questions to consider: Who owns this collection of student work? Who has had input? Who has selected the work that goes in it? What is the home situation for this child? As teachers, we need to be sensitive to a variety of issues. We each need to consider what our issues are.

Teacher: "I'm always struggling with myself. It is so tempting to take my students' collections of work and make them over to satisfy myself."

Teachers are learning that when they assume control over students' work, students cease to have ownership—and commitment.

COLLECTING EVIDENCE OF LEARNING—KEEPING FOCUSED

TEACHER CONSIDERATIONS	RESPONSE
1. How have I involved the students in the process of collecting evidence of their learning? ✐ Are they given time to practice sharing their learning with parents? ✐ Have there been opportunities for rehearsal with peers and older student buddies? ✐ Do students feel that they "own" their own collections of work? ✐ Have they been given the freedom and opportunity to select what is important to them? ✐ How have I helped children see the range of evidence and what it signifies in terms of their learning?	
2. How have I involved the parents in the process of collecting evidence of their children's learning? ✐ Have I asked parents what is important to them? Have I asked them what they would like to see more of in these collections of work? ✐ How have I helped parents comment on their children's work? ✐ How have I helped them "see" the learning that is developing? ✐ How can I encourage parents to work with their children and select something from home to insert into the collection of work?	
3. How are we collaborating as a staff? ✐ Have we taken time for discussions about the collection of work for evidence: of finding out what evidence of learning looks like and how we might collect it? ✐ How can we make connections with both parents of a child if they are living apart? ✐ How can we use collections of work to inform the following year's teacher? ✐ How are we as a staff modeling the building of collections of work by collecting and sharing our work as teachers?	

Continued next page

TEACHER CONSIDERATIONS	RESPONSE
4. How am I preparing myself for three-way reporting? ✐ What have I given up doing so that I have the time to take on this process? ✐ Have I set up a system to make the collection of student work accessible and easy to manage? ✐ Am I trying to do too much too soon? Should I start with one focus area or subject? ✐ What things do I really need more time to talk about? ✐ Can I articulate why collecting evidence is important in the process of student learning?	

EVIDENCE OF LEARNING—TOGETHER IS BETTER

TOGETHER IS BETTER: When students are involved in collecting evidence of their own learning, they begin to identify and value their own strengths and to probe and search those areas that need improvement. Through the "pictures" that these collections of work give, teachers and parents have more insight into the learners' growth and development.

Student Reflection

Reflection is thinking—about what you've done, what you've tried to do, and how you feel about what you've done.

Student reflection can be

-  students circling favorite sentences
- students selecting work and writing "two stars and a wish"
- students telling their partners two things that they want them to notice about their paintings
- students writing in their thinking logs at the end of the day about three things they have learned and two questions they still have
- students telling their partners how they arrived at their answers in mathematics
- students talking individually with their teacher about their research projects, explaining what it is they are trying to do, and suggesting one way their teacher, or another person, could help them

When we encourage children to think and talk about their learning, we are providing them with valuable insights. We are also giving children opportunities to extend their understanding of their own learning. While student reflection is not a complicated process, time and practice are essential if it is going to become a positive learning habit.

A SNAPSHOT OF STUDENT REFLECTION

1. Talk with students about the purpose and importance of reflection.

2. Model what learners do when they reflect: pose questions, think aloud, self-monitor, change what they do as a result.

3. Provide opportunities for oral rehearsal and working together as a class to develop vocabulary.

4. Provide opportunities to practice both as individuals and with others—sometimes orally and sometimes in writing.

STUDENT REFLECTION—TEACHER-PROVEN IDEAS

Some colleagues have described the following ideas for developing and encouraging student reflection that were successful for them.

Idea! Modeling Reflection for Your Students   88
Idea! Providing for Oral Rehearsal   89
Idea! Reflecting with a Partner   90
Idea! Encouraging Student Self-reflection   91
Idea! Getting Specific   92
Idea! Recording Reflections   93
Idea! Adding to the Collections of Students' Work   94
Idea! Including Parents   95
Idea! Recording Memorable Moments   96
Idea! Giving Specific Compliments   97
Idea! The Week in Review   98

IDEA!

MODELING REFLECTION FOR YOUR STUDENTS

One teacher uses thought clouds to make her own thinking explicit to her students. Following the completion of hands-on science experiments, the teacher recorded the following thought cloud on the board.

After doing this on a regular basis with her students, she now draws blank thought clouds and invites students to contribute their thoughts. The teacher notes these down for the students, as the purpose is not to practice writing but rather to demonstrate the basic habit of thinking about thinking.

IDEA!

PROVIDING FOR ORAL REHEARSAL

A teacher gives her young students numerous opportunities to practice reflection orally. One of their favorite activities takes place at the end of the lesson when the teacher holds the "thinking rock" and tells the students that when they hold the rock they can tell one thing they have learned or share one question. Students always have the option to pass.

The teacher starts the process by saying, "Today in math I learned that..." She then turns and passes the rock to the student on the right.

She uses different leads such as

- One thing I found really hard today...
- Something I never did before was...
- I'm still wondering about...
- I feel _____ when...

As she varies the leads, students are able to increase their own vocabularies as well as practice articulating their thoughts about their learning.

IDEA!

REFLECTING WITH A PARTNER

A teacher whose students have just finished making dioramas asks each of her students to turn to a classmate and tell two things they liked about their own diorama and one wish for a change if they could do it over again. The teacher found that once students were familiar with reflection, some students got into the habit of taking their work to a friend, a visitor, or class buddy and sharing two stars and a wish with them.

IDEA!

ENCOURAGING STUDENT SELF-REFLECTION

One teacher encouraged student self-reflection in the following way. Whenever students came to him and asked, "Do you like it?" or "Is it okay?" the teacher turned the questions back to the students by saying, "Yes. I'll tell you something about it if you'll

- ✐ tell me two things that you like about it."
- ✐ tell me *your* two stars and a wish about your work."
- ✐ tell me what is important to you."
- ✐ tell me one piece of advice that you would give someone else working on a similar project."

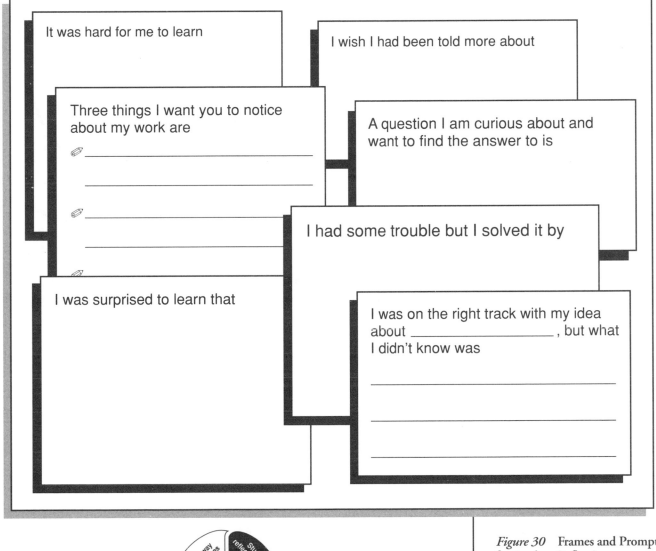

> It was hard for me to learn
>
> I wish I had been told more about
>
> Three things I want you to notice about my work are
> ✐ _____
> _____
> ✐ _____
> _____
> ✐ _____
>
> A question I am curious about and want to find the answer to is
>
> I had some trouble but I solved it by
>
> I was surprised to learn that
>
> I was on the right track with my idea about _____ , but what I didn't know was
> _____
> _____
> _____

Figure 30   Frames and Prompts for Student Reflection

Blackline master in Appendix C.

GETTING SPECIFIC

After small-group book sharing, one teacher, whose students were having a great deal of difficulty getting beyond comments like "It was great!" or "I liked it," helped them become more specific in their thinking about their reading. Together with the class, the teacher developed two circles of different colors that described how they used their own reading time.

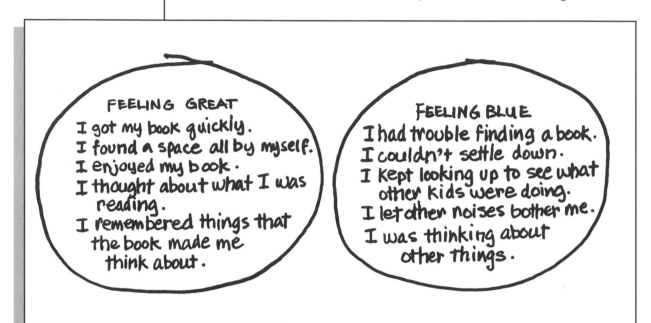

After they had developed the circles, the teacher would say, "Let's take a minute and think about what color you are today. Who would like to tell me what color you are and one reason why?" This strategy also helps children think about their learning in any subject area.

IDEA!

RECORDING REFLECTIONS

One teacher, just before break time, would ask her students to fill in an "Exit Pass," which included simple frames such as

- ✐ One thing I learned today was...
- ✐ Something I'm going to tell everyone at the dinner table is...
- ✐ Two questions I have about what we were working on today are...

She asked students to hand these to her on their way out the door. Later she made quick comments on them and handed them back to students to put in their collections of work.

Figure 31   Exit Pass

IDEA!

ADDING TO THE COLLECTIONS OF STUDENTS' WORK

Every Friday, during the last thirty minutes, one teacher has students go to their folders to find samples of their work to glue into their scrapbooks or to put into their portfolios. He may ask them to choose something that they are really proud of that they did that week. They insert that piece and add a note telling of two things that they want the reader to notice about their work and one goal that they have for "next time." The teacher varies what he asks the students to select, asking them to select according to different categories, for example, a piece that shows risk-taking or problem-solving or collaboration, a piece they want to fix at a later date, or a piece they want to burn.

It wasn't long before each student in this class was able to select a piece of work and explain why he or she had chosen it. Once students were comfortable with this, the teacher regularly asked them to make independent selections according to their criteria.

The teacher photocopies a variety of different forms and provides students with a small glue stick to let them make their own sticky notes.

This piece is an example of…

I want you to notice…

Date _____   _____

[Signature]

Figure 32
Student-made Sticky Notes

IDEA!

INCLUDING PARENTS

To help parents understand and appreciate their children being engaged in reflection, one teacher sent home the following letter:

Dear Parent(s)—

In all our classroom activities, students are encouraged to talk about what they have learned, how they have learned it, the successes they've had, the questions they're asking, and the things they want to improve.

One way you could encourage this process of student reflection is to try some dinner-time dynamics. Here are some questions you might ask:

- What did you do today that really made you think?
- What is one problem you had, and how did you solve it?
- What did you do today that made you laugh?
- What is something that you are getting better at doing?
- Who are three people who can help you if you need help?

Remember to take part in the conversations yourself and encourage other family members to take a turn. We hope your dinner conversations will change from, "What did you do today at school?" "Nothing," to something much more enjoyable and informative for everyone.

Best wishes

Figure 33   Letter Requesting That Parents Help Their Children Reflect

IDEA!

RECORDING MEMORABLE MOMENTS

To provide a cumulative record of each child's year, one teacher had students use special notebooks for this purpose. Each week, each child recorded his or her most memorable moment and selected something to symbolize that moment—a photograph, a picture, a piece of work. Sometimes a child's highlight of the week was something that had occurred outside school—earning a swimming badge, winning a soccer game, completing a babysitter's course successfully.

Another teacher asked children to describe in their notebooks how they felt on the first day of school and how they felt now that the first month of school was coming to an end.

> The thing that was special for me this week was
>
> and I want to remember it because

Feelings—then and now

On the first day of school I feelt happy becaues I was agoing to met new friends. I was wried becaues I was going to get all of are school soping don. I was nrvis becaues I was going to a new school. Now I have friends. Now I have most of my school soping. Now I'm at a new school and I am happy.

Figure 34
Feelings Then and Now

GIVING SPECIFIC COMPLIMENTS

To help children become specific in their observations, one teacher takes advantage of his students' love of dramatization. He follows each dramatization with an invitation to them to give specific compliments to each of the players. For example, following the dramatization of Cinderella, the compliments given to the stepsisters were:

"I liked the way that Lianne kept her mouth turned down and her nose wrinkled the whole time."

"It was good the way Chelsea made the stepsister sound mean without screaming at us. She just lowered her voice."

THE WEEK IN REVIEW

Establishing a time to reflect weekly helps students focus on their learning and provide a record of their learning in a year. One teacher uses the following form, asking students to take it home and share it with parents. The weekly reflections are kept with students' collections of work. Another teacher chooses to have children reflect on their projects work experience.

THE WEEK IN REVIEW

_____ Date

This week I feel good about _____

_____

_____

_____

_____

me because _____

_____

I really had to work on _____

_____

I had fun when _____

_____

My goal next week is to _____

_____

_____

Signed,

_____

Name _____   **Date** _____

PROJECT PROFILE

What I did	
How I did it	
How I feel	
Who I worked with	
A highlight for me	
What's next	

Figure 35A
The Week In Review

Figure 35B
Project Profile

Blackline masters in Appendix C.

LEARNING FROM LISTENING

As we listen to the comments of students, parents, and teachers, we continue to learn more about the process.

Student: "I like getting time to think and to look through what we've done. It lets me see that I'm really learning something."

Students who have time to reflect on their learning have time to appreciate what they have learned. They are able to set new goals knowing that they are capable of meeting them.

Parent: "I used to be so frustrated when all Norman could answer in response to questions about school was, "Nothing." Now he is able to tell me what he is learning and what he wants to learn. It's amazing."

Parents appreciate being involved in their child's learning. Finding ways to help children share what they know builds stronger connections among parents, their children, and teachers.

Teacher: "It's hard to believe that having students reflecting on their learning would make such a difference. Last year it was hard to get the students to talk about their learning during our three-way conferences. This year they can be specific about what they're learning."

Articulating our understanding about what we have learned prepares us to share our learning with others. It takes practice.

Teacher: "I never realized how many 'secrets' I had. I never thought to share, in any real detail, why we were doing things the way we did. I guess I thought it was obvious. I guessed wrong. Now that I'm telling the kids *why* I want them to do things, they seem to be learning faster."

If we know where we're going and how we're expected to get there, we are able to make better decisions along the way. Sharing our goals with students allows them to throw their energy towards learning. Rather than waiting for us to lead them, they are able to lead themselves.

STUDENT REFLECTION—KEEPING FOCUSED

TEACHER CONSIDERATIONS	RESPONSE

1. How have I involved the students in the process of reflection?
   ✐ Have they had time and practice in reflecting about their learning?
   ✐ How have I provided a risk-taking environment?
   ✐ Do they understand why they are reflecting?
   ✐ How am I modeling my own reflection about my learning in the classroom?
   ✐ How am I helping them build their own vocabularies to express themselves?	

2. How have I involved the parents in the process of student reflection?
   ✐ Have I informed them about the process of reflection and how we will be using it in the classroom?
   ✐ Have I encouraged appropriate parent responses that validate what students are doing?	

3. How are we collaborating as a staff?
   ✐ Have we taken time for discussions about what reflection is and what it can look like in our classrooms?
   ✐ Are we as a staff modeling by reflecting on our own decisions and how we work with students?	

4. How am I preparing myself for having students use reflection?
   ✐ What have I given up doing so that I have the time to take on this process?
   ✐ What are the things that I really need more time to talk about?
   ✐ What is my major concern? What am I feeling most comfortable with?
   ✐ Have I found the balance—is there too much or too little reflection?
   ✐ Can I articulate why reflection is important in the process of student learning?	

STUDENT REFLECTION—TOGETHER IS BETTER

TOGETHER IS BETTER: Teachers and parents, by supporting and helping children articulate their learning, help them develop self-direction and autonomy. Reflection helps students gain a sense of what they can do and what they can improve upon. In this way, students, by knowing what they value in their work, become contributors to the evaluation process.

Conclusion: Creating a Collaborative Environment

The ideas and suggestions contained in this book reflect three years of working with students, parents, and teachers in a variety of schools and districts. As teachers work to create a collaborative environment, new roles are emerging.

Now that teachers know so much more about how children learn, we are shifting our view of the role of students from passive recipients of knowledge to active participants in their own learning. Participation in the three-way reporting process allows children to understand themselves better as learners and to begin to exert more control over *what* they are learning and *how* they are learning it. This process encourages students to monitor their own learning and, as a result, adjust what they are doing in terms of their own expectations of themselves and their understanding of what teachers and parents expect for them. Students cannot do this alone.

Parents provide essential support for students' learning. They are responsible for their children's safety and well-being as well as their growth towards independence and adulthood. Learning and growing are the processes that we as individuals undergo as we make the change from dependence to independence. Teachers and parents work together to help students to reach independence: independence as learners—independence as citizens.

We are seeking ways to work with our students' parents, recognizing that they are essential partners in framing the shape of the reporting process. As teachers engaged in the process of three-way reporting, we have an opportunity to invite, include, and inform parents—and to allow them to inform us.

The implementation of any changes in assessment, evaluation, and reporting takes time and involves working with our colleagues, our students, and their parents. Teachers, working with each other, provide the support necessary to change our established ways of doing things—in this case, our assessment, evaluation, and reporting processes. We encourage you to work together to undertake these changes.

The kinds of partnerships we have described in this book are based upon changing our relationships with students and parents. Our ultimate goal is to enhance students' learning and ensure continuing success because **TOGETHER IS BETTER.**

Appendix A:
Anecdotal Reports

GUIDELINES FOR WRITING AN EFFECTIVE ANECDOTAL REPORT

1. Begin with student successes.
2. State concerns and include an action plan.
3. Tell about the whole child.
4. Use clear language (avoid teacher jargon).
5. Be specific and include examples whenever possible.
6. Highlight the uniqueness of each child. (Parents have reminded us how important it is to them that our descriptions of learning recognize the uniqueness of their children and that we not use comments that could apply to any child in the class.)

BEGIN WITH STUDENT SUCCESSES

What this might look like:

PRIMARY

> R. continues to be a most thoughtful student. This is apparent when she gives positive, specific compliments to others at Reading Club. She chooses a variety of books and is able to retell any story. When reading books at her ability level, books such as *Cat and Mouse* or *When Itchy Witchy Sneezes*, she reads from memory and goes back to correct any perceived mistakes.
>
> The most dramatic breakthrough is R.'s growing ability in writing. She has moved from copying words and using strings of letters to making a good match between sounds and letters, e.g., "I PLAYEF MI DOLS." R. is a hard worker who is willing to put a lot of effort into doing a good job.
>
> R. is able to match and record numbers to 20. She can sort objects and extend a repeated pattern. R.'s independence is shown by the way she initiates arts and crafts activities. She is never at a loss for something to do and has a wide range of ideas and strategies for creating projects. All of the successes outlined in this report shows what a conscientious self-directed learner she is.

INTERMEDIATE

When I think of Adrian, I immediately imagine a "doer." He enjoys all subject areas and likes to be involved in something "new" at all times. I was impressed with his original project on the environment—not only for his knowledge of the subject, but also for his insight into the issues.

STATE CONCERNS AND INCLUDE AN ACTION PLAN

What this might look like:

PRIMARY

As we've discussed, I am concerned that A. continues to be so hard on himself about standard spelling. I have explained to him that it is most important that he get his ideas down and that it is OK for five-year-olds to put down all the letters they think make up a word. I will continue to encourage him to take the risk of trying his own spellings, and I will make sure that he has plenty of scrap paper to use for "first tries."

A. has agreed to try spelling words by himself before coming to ask for help. Any opportunities for writing (e.g., grocery lists, reminders) that you can give A. would be welcomed.

INTERMEDIATE

Alison does not apply the rules of capitalization, sentence structure, and punctuation in her written assignments in social studies and science. I know that she has an understanding of these rules (she scored 18/20 on a recent proofreading quiz); she simply neglects to apply them. I have asked Alison to focus on one or two aspects at a time (e.g., to work only on improved capitalization). Alison has agreed to proofread all homework assignments before handing them in. The importance of being able to produce an error-free published piece will be highlighted when we work on next term's project display in the library.

TELL ABOUT THE WHOLE CHILD

What this might look like:

PRIMARY

S. is a hard worker with ideas to share and a helping hand for anyone who needs it. This was obvious when he was a major contributor to the racing car and board projects. His initiative was evident when he brought materials and took part in designing such things as a steering wheel and axles. S. makes excellent use of his time.

OR

L. continues to be a leader in our class. She can be counted on to enter all activities with enthusiasm. I appreciate her willingness and ability to help other children. In gym she is a popular partner because she works well with others and has many ideas for designing games.

INTERMEDIATE

Gordon is cooperative in group activities and gets along well with others in the class. He brought his musical drama expertise from his work in community productions to our school's version of *The Mikado*.

USE CLEAR LANGUAGE (AVOID TEACHER JARGON)

What this might look like:

PRIMARY

M. is becoming better able to express his ideas in writing. There isn't much he can't write if someone sits with him and acts as a coach. Given his age this is most appropriate. With continued support we are confident that he will become increasingly independent. His ability to make good approximations of standard spelling is apparent when he writes "IM PROUD OF MI SWMING."

INTERMEDIATE

During our daily fifteen minute reading time, [jargon: U.S.S.R.; D.E.A.R.; S.S.R.], Randy is absorbed by a new book almost every week. Right now, his preferred author is Eric Wilson.

BE SPECIFIC AND INCLUDE EXAMPLES WHENEVER POSSIBLE

What this might look like:

PRIMARY

A. is at a stage in writing where she is most comfortable copying words or getting help from others, but I am seeing breakthroughs into independence such as "Alison GoS two PeaNo!" (Alison goes to piano).

INTERMEDIATE

In math, Angie listens carefully to instruction, follows directions, and then promptly begins the assigned task. She is now able to multiply by two-digit numbers (e.g., 117 x 37) and divide confidently with a one-digit divisor (e.g., 481 ÷ 8). A recent problem set is attached to show you her improvement in these areas.

HIGHLIGHT THE UNIQUENESS OF EACH CHILD

What this might look like:

PRIMARY

When asked to write what he wanted to be included on his report card, P. composed the following message on the computer, "I woat you to rit me im got at york." I agree, and my goal for P. is for him to keep being the marvelous worker he is.

INTERMEDIATE

One of the things we appreciate about S. is the way he always adds a comment to our discussion that gives us a different way of thinking about the topic.

OR

I am impressed by the way in which Elizabeth manages to go to her piano lessons and rehearsals each week and still produce such quality school work. Her commitment to excellence carries through in everything that she does.

OR

The entire class was very interested in hearing about Candice's involvement with and interest in skateboarding. Her presentation gave us first-hand information about the different types of tricks and boards.

Appendix B:
Suggested Resources

The way we view assessment and evaluation of student learning has changed, and in times of change we learn. The following books are excellent resources that contributed to our learning.

Becoming Responsible Learners by Mark Collis and Joan Dalton, published by Heinemann (1990).

Evaluating Literacy by R. Anthony, T. Johnson, N. Mickelson, A. Preece, published by Heinemann (1991).

Expanding Student Assessment edited by V. Perrone, published by the Association for Supervision and Curriculum Development (1991).

If Minds Matter–Vol.II edited by Arthur Costa, James Bellanca, and Robin Fogarty ("Finding Out What We Need to Know" by Sharon Jeroski and "How Do We Know We're Getting Better" by Sharon Jeroski and Faye Brownlie), published by Skylight Publishing (1992).

Invitations: Changing as Teachers and Learners K–12 by R. Routman, published by Heinemann (1991).

Looking, Listening, and Learning: Observing and Assessing Young Readers by Carl Braun, published by Peguis Publishers (1993).

Making Connections: Teaching and the Human Brain by R. Caine and G. Caine, published by the Association for Supervision and Curriculum Development (1991).

Reading : What Can Be Measured? by R. Farr and R. Carey, published by the International Reading Association (1986).

Tests: Marked for Life by S. Alan Cohen, a Bright Idea Book, published by Scholastic (1988).

Appendix C:
Blackline Masters

THREE-WAY CONFERENCE GUIDE FOR TEACHERS

Student's name

Date

Areas of strength	Areas needing improvement
Notes for the conference	Additional notes

Action Plan
Goal:

Student will...	Teacher will...	Parent will...

Other notes:

THREE-WAY CONFERENCE GUIDE FOR STUDENTS

_____   _____
Name   **Date**

Two things I need to improve…

Things to show…

My next term goal is…

CLASS RECORD SHEET		
The goal	Evidence of meeting the goal	Resetting the goal

PARENT RESPONSE TO CONFERENCE

What we liked about the conference: _____

_____

_____

_____

_____

What we need to know more about: _____

_____

_____

_____

_____

Two suggestions for the next conference: _____

_____

_____

_____

_____

Other comments? _____

_____

_____

_____

_____

_____

_____

_____

_____

VIDEO VIEWING GUIDE

This is our class at work. We are _____

_____

_____

We also are _____

_____

Three key points I want to stress are _____

_____

_____

_____

_____

Enjoy the video!   _____

                                              [Teacher's name]

Viewers' Responses—We invite your comments!

Comments	Signature

Figure 13, page 51, "Video Viewing Guide."
From *Together Is Better* by Davies/Cameron/Politano/Gregory © Peguis Publishers, 1992. This page may be reproduced for classroom use.

PARENT RESPONSE SHEET FOR PORTFOLIO REVIEW

Comments

What two things would you like to have included in the next portfolio?

1. _____

_____

_____

_____

2. _____

_____

_____

_____

Signature(s) _____

_____

PARENT RESPONSE SHEET FOR PORTFOLIO REVIEW
Portfolio Review

Date _____

Name _____

Two Stars

★

★

One Wish

Dear _____
           [Student's name]

In looking at your work so far, I/we would like to compliment you on

_____

_____

_____

_____

The most important thing I/we would like to say to you now is

_____

_____

_____

As your parent(s), I/we _____

_____

_____

_____

                    _____
                              [Parent's signature]

                    _____
                              [Parent's signature]

P.S. Dear _____
              [Teacher's name]

I/we would like to let you know that _____

_____

_____

MY INFORMAL REPORT TO MY PARENT(S)

Date _____ Name _____

1. The most important thing in our classroom that I am trying to do well is _____

_____

_____

2. This is important to me because _____

_____

_____

3. Two things that I have done well this term are _____

_____

_____

4. One thing that I need to work harder at is _____

_____

_____

5. Something that I am proud about this term is _____

_____

_____

6. My goal(s) for next term is (are) _____

_____

_____

7. Attached are some samples of my work. Please notice that _____

_____

_____

_____
[Student's signature]

Figure 18B, page 58, "Informal Report to Parents (Example 2—Side 1)."
From *Together Is Better* by Davies/Cameron/Politano/Gregory © Peguis Publishers, 1992. This page may be reproduced for classroom use.

PARENT'S RESPONSE

1. _____ , I compliment you on your work sample. I especially liked

_____

_____

_____

2. One thing I would like you to work on is _____

_____

_____

_____

3. During our three-way conference in November I would like to know more about

_____

_____

_____

_____
[Parent's signature]

Name _____

Age _____ Date _____

Teacher(s) _____

_____

Child's comments _____

_____

_____

_____

_____

Teacher(s) comments _____

_____

_____

_____

Parent(s) comments _____

_____

_____

_____

_____

Figure 18D, page 60, "Informal Report to Parents (Example 4)."
From *Together Is Better* by Davies/Cameron/Politano/Gregory © Peguis Publishers, 1992. This page may be reproduced for classroom use.

Language Arts

INFORMATION SHEET

Prior to finalizing my long-range plans for this year, I would appreciate information from you regarding your child's perceived strengths and needs.

As parent(s) you are in the best position to evaluate your child's use of language and language skills (such as reading and writing) in "the real world." I would appreciate your consideration of the following questions and your careful appraisal of your child's skills.

Thank you!

_____
[Teacher's signature]

✎ We/I would like our child to learn _____ this year. We/I would like our child to be exposed to _____ and _____ .

_____ is particularly good at _____ and _____ . He/she is also able to _____ easily. However, in spite of _____ 's talents, _____ needs lots of assistance to _____ and _____ .

✎ In general, a perfect Language Arts program for _____ would _____ _____ _____ .

✎ If you ever want _____ 's undivided attention you just have to mention _____ or _____ . But whatever you do, don't ever mention _____ !!

Good luck in your endeavors!!   Sincerely,

                                        _____

                                        _____ 's parent(s)

Figure 19, page 62, "Information from Parents."
From *Together Is Better* by Davies/Cameron/Politano/Gregory © Peguis Publishers, 1992. This page may be reproduced for classroom use.

One thing I like…	One thing I need to change…
One thing my parent(s) would really like about this piece…	One thing my teacher would notice about my writing is…

An effective project includes...

✏ _____ ☐　　✏ _____ ☐

✏ _____ ☐　　✏ _____ ☐

✏ _____ ☐　　✏ _____ ☐

✏ _____ ☐　　✏ _____ ☐

You can see I know this because...

_____

_____

_____

_____

_____

_____

_____

_____

When I chose to include this example of my writing in my portfolio I remembered that…

Fiction

✐ _____
✐ _____
✐ _____
✐ _____
✐ _____
✐ _____

Non-fiction

✐ _____
✐ _____
✐ _____
✐ _____
✐ _____
✐ _____

I also know that it is important that my work is neat and that it has been edited for spelling and sentence structure.

The piece of work I have chosen is…

It shows…

I want you to notice…

Please give me one compliment and ask me one question after you read my selection.

I put this in my portfolio on _____ _____

[date]   [signature]

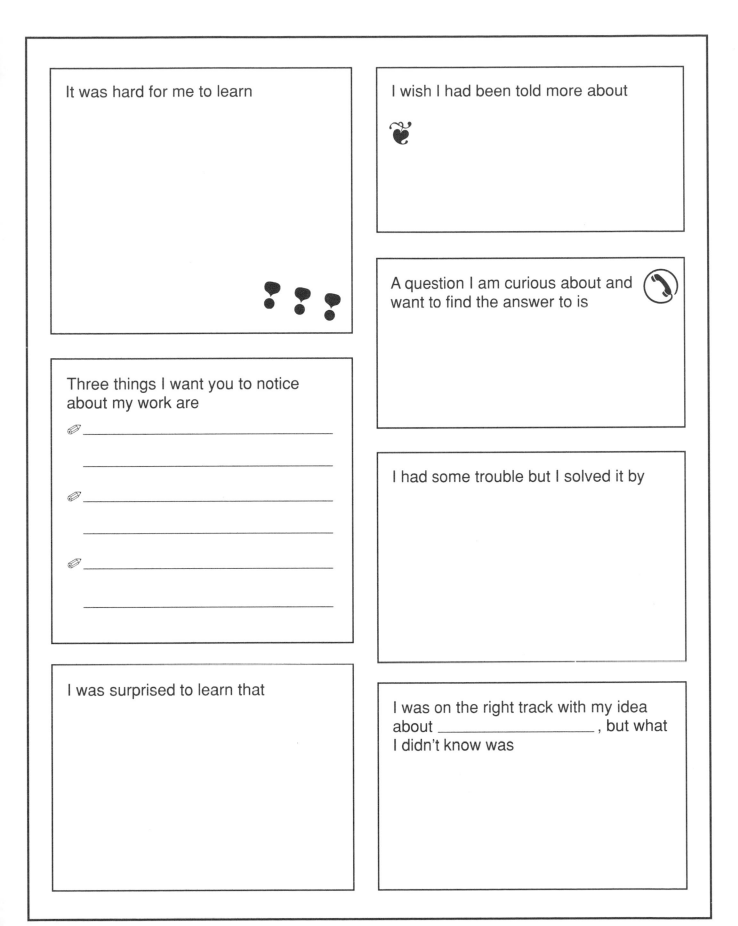

It was hard for me to learn

I wish I had been told more about

A question I am curious about and want to find the answer to is

Three things I want you to notice about my work are

_____

_____

_____

I had some trouble but I solved it by

I was surprised to learn that

I was on the right track with my idea about _____ , but what I didn't know was

_____
Date

THE WEEK IN REVIEW

This week I feel good about _____

_____ because

_____

_____ was easy for

me because _____

_____

I really had to work on _____

_____

I had fun when _____

_____

My goal next week is to _____

_____

_____

Signed,

_____

Name ——————————————— **Date** ———————————

PROJECT PROFILE

What I did	
How I did it	
How I feel	
Who I worked with	
A highlight for me	
What's next	